HISTORY OF
RUSSIA

The Complete Story of Empire, Revolution, and Power from Ancient Rus to the Modern Age

SAMUEL CORWIN

Copyright © 2026 by Samuel Corwin. All rights reserved.

No part of this publication may be reproduced, distributed, or transmitted in any form or by any means, including photocopying, recording, or other electronic or mechanical methods, without the prior written permission of the publisher, except in the case of brief quotations embodied in critical reviews and certain other noncommercial uses permitted by copyright law.

This book may contain illustrations, maps, or visual reconstructions generated or enhanced with the assistance of artificial intelligence (AI) technology for educational, illustrative, and historical clarification purposes. These visuals are intended to help bring historical events, places, and figures to life for readers.

This book is intended for informational and educational purposes only. While every effort has been made to ensure the accuracy of the information contained herein, the author makes no representations or warranties regarding the completeness or accuracy of the contents and assumes no responsibility for any errors or omissions.

The information in this book is not intended to provide legal, financial, or professional advice.

All historical interpretations and opinions expressed in this book are those of the author and do not necessarily reflect the views of any institutions or organizations.

Table of Contents

Introduction
The Country That Refuses to End

On a winter morning in 1991, the red flag came down over the Kremlin and a different flag went up, and a state that had spanned eleven time zones, fought two world wars, and put the first human into orbit simply stopped existing. There was no surrender, no foreign army at the gates, no signed instrument of capitulation. The Soviet Union dissolved by paperwork. Within a few years, foreign observers were writing obituaries for Russian power, and Russians themselves were burying parents in cemeteries where the headstones still bore the hammer and sickle.

And then, slowly at first and then with startling speed, the country came back.

This is the pattern. Kievan Rus collapsed under the Mongols and a new Russia rose around Moscow. The Romanov dynasty ended in a basement in Yekaterinburg and a new Russia rose around Lenin. The Soviet experiment ended with a stroke of a pen in a Belarusian forest and a new Russia rose around Putin. Each time the obituary is filed, a new chapter begins. Each new Russia denounces the one before it, and each new Russia carries it anyway - in the street names it cannot bring itself to change, in the borders it refuses to relinquish, in the arguments it has with itself about what it is.

A Civilization Between Worlds

In June 2008, the newly elected Russian president Dmitry Medvedev stood at a podium in Berlin and told his audience that the Cold War had ended in a particular way: with the defeat of one side, and with the victorious side then refusing to admit that the world had changed. He spoke calmly. He wore a good suit. He used the language of European diplomacy. But the argument underneath the language was older than the building he was standing in. Russia, he was saying, was not a junior partner to be lectured. It was a civilization in its own right.

This claim - that Russia is not a country but a civilization - has a long pedigree. In the nineteenth century, Nikolai Danilevsky argued that history did not move along a single track toward a single destination called the modern West, but that distinct civilizational types each followed their own paths and had their own seasons. Konstantin Leontiev pushed the argument further, suspicious of European liberalism and convinced that Russia's destiny lay in its difference. In our own time, the philosopher Alexander Dugin has rebuilt the same scaffolding for a different audience, and Russia's foreign minister Sergei Lavrov has spoken of a model of human development distinct from the Western one.

The argument is not new. What is striking is how durable it is. Russian intellectuals have been having this fight - are we European, are we Asian, are we something else entirely - for at least three hundred years. Peter the Great shaved the boyars' beards and built a city on a swamp because he believed Russia had to become European or die. Slavophiles in the nineteenth century answered that Russia's salvation lay precisely in not becoming European. Communists declared they were building something beyond both East and West. Post-Soviet liberals in the 1990s tried to rejoin what they called the civilized world. By the 2000s, the wheel had turned again.

An outsider can find this dizzying. Why does the question never settle? Part of the answer is that Russia genuinely sits between two worlds. Its early princes took their Christianity from Constantinople, not Rome. Its medieval centuries were spent under the rule of a Mongol khan whose capital was on the Volga. Its modern empire pushed east into Siberia and the Pacific while its court read French novels and danced French quadrilles. To stand in Kazan, where the muezzin calls over the Kremlin walls, or in Vladivostok, which is closer to Tokyo than to Moscow, is to feel the question physically. The country is not pretending to be uncertain about its identity. It is uncertain about its identity.

The Questions This Book Asks

A history of Russia could be written as a story of rulers, or of revolutions, or of wars, or of writers. All of those books exist and many are excellent. The book in your hands tries to do something a little different. It treats Russian history as a long argument the country has been having with itself, and it tries to follow the argument from its medieval origins to the wars and crises of our own decade.

Four questions run through the chapters that follow.

The first is the question of what Russia is. Is it a European country that took some wrong turns, an Asian country with a European veneer, a civilization unto itself, or simply an empire that has never figured out how to become a nation? Different Russians at different times have answered all four. The answer matters because it shapes everything else - whom Russia trusts, whom it fights, what laws it writes, what stories it tells its children.

The second is the question of how Russia is governed. From the grand princes of Moscow to the general secretaries of the Politburo, power in Russia has tended to concentrate in a single figure at the top and to radiate outward through a hierarchy of personal loyalties rather than impersonal institutions. Reformers have tried again and again to change this, and again and again the old pattern has reasserted itself. Why?

The third is the question of Russia and the world. The country has been invaded from almost every direction - by Mongols from the east, by Poles and Swedes and French and Germans from the west, by Turks from the south. It has also been one of history's great invaders, pushing its borders outward in every direction across four centuries. The relationship between Russian insecurity and Russian aggression is not simple, and neither side of it can be understood without the other.

The fourth is the question of the Russian people themselves - the peasants who made up the overwhelming majority of the population until the twentieth century, the workers who built the Soviet cities, the intelligentsia who argued in cramped apartments about how to save the country, the soldiers who died in numbers that other societies find almost incomprehensible. A history that tracks only the men in the Kremlin misses most of what actually happened.

These questions do not have clean answers. But they are better than the alternative, which is to treat Russia as a riddle wrapped in an enigma and then throw up one's hands. Russia is not a riddle. It is a country with a history, and the history is knowable.

Geography as Destiny

Open a map. The first thing you notice about Russia is that there is too much of it. From the Baltic to the Pacific is nearly six thousand miles. A train from Moscow to Vladivostok takes a week. The country contains tundra and desert, swamp and steppe, taiga that stretches farther than the eye or the mind can follow. No other nation has had to govern so much space with so little of it useful for growing food.

The second thing you notice is the absence of natural borders. Western Europe has the Alps and the Pyrenees, the Channel and the Mediterranean. China has the Himalayas and the Gobi. Russia, on the great Eurasian plain, has almost nothing. The land rolls open from the Carpathians to the Urals without serious interruption, and the Urals themselves are low, worn-down mountains a cavalry force can ride around. Anyone who wants to invade Russia from the west has a highway. Anyone who wants to invade Europe from Russia has the same highway in reverse.

This single fact has shaped Russian history more than any ruler. A country without defensible frontiers learns to keep its enemies as far from its capital as possible, which means pushing the frontier outward, which means acquiring neighbors, which means acquiring their neighbors in turn. Russian expansion has been driven by hunger for warm-water ports and trade routes and the wealth of new lands, but underneath all of those motives sits a simpler one: the desire to never again be where the Mongols found Kiev in 1240, or where Napoleon found Moscow in 1812, or where the Wehrmacht found itself in the suburbs of the capital in 1941.

The rivers, meanwhile, did the opposite work. The Volga, the Dnieper, the Don, the Northern Dvina - these were the highways of medieval Rus, the arteries along which furs and slaves and silver moved between the Baltic and the Black Sea, between Scandinavia and Byzantium. The earliest Russian state grew along a river route. Later, the same waterways carried grain to the cities and tied the provinces to Moscow. When Peter the Great wanted a new capital, he built it where a river met the sea.

Geography is not destiny in the strict sense. People make choices, and the same landscape can produce different histories under different leaders. But geography is the room in which the choices are made, and the room in Russia's case is very large, very flat, very cold, and very exposed.

Scope, Sources, and Approach

This book begins in the ninth century, when a confederation of Slavic tribes and Scandinavian traders coalesced around the river towns of what is now Ukraine, Belarus, and western Russia, and when a princess named Olga, widowed and dangerous, began the slow work of turning a tribute-collecting racket into something resembling a state. It ends in the present, with a Russia at war in Ukraine and engaged in a confrontation with the West that few would have predicted a generation ago.

Between those two points lie a thousand years. No single volume can cover all of it in full, and this one does not try. The chapters that follow move at different speeds. Some pause on a single reign or a single decade because that is where the country was being remade. Others compress a century into a few pages because the country was, for a while, doing what it had been doing before. The aim is not coverage but understanding.

The sources behind the book are the standard ones a general history rests on: the chronicles of medieval Rus, the dispatches of foreign ambassadors, the memoirs of statesmen and revolutionaries, the work of Russian and Western historians who have spent their careers in the archives. Where the evidence is contested - and on questions of Russian history it very often is - the text says so. Historians differ, for example, on how much the Mongol yoke actually shaped later Russian autocracy, on what Ivan the Terrible's terror was really for, on whether the 1917 revolution was inevitable or contingent. On such questions the honest answer is to lay out the disagreement rather than pretend it does not exist.

A note on names and dates. Russian names have been transliterated in the forms most familiar to English readers - Tsar Alexei rather than Aleksei, Trotsky rather than Trotskii. Dates before 1918 are given in the old Julian calendar when that is how the participants experienced them, with the modern equivalent noted where confusion is likely. Place names follow the usage of the time: Petersburg becomes Petrograd in 1914 and Leningrad in 1924 and

Petersburg again in 1991, and the text moves with it. The approach throughout is narrative. People do things, and other things happen as a result. The analysis is woven into the story rather than broken out into separate boxes. A reader who finishes the book should come away not with a list of dates but with a feel for the country - its rhythms, its obsessions, its repeated mistakes, its astonishing creativity, the texture of life inside it.

The Road Ahead

The story begins on a river, with a band of Scandinavian traders who would have been astonished to learn that the territory they were passing through would one day be the largest country on earth. It moves through the rise and ruin of Kievan Rus, through two and a half centuries under the Mongols, through the gathering of the Russian lands around a small wooden fortress on the Moscow River. It follows Ivan the Terrible into madness, Peter the Great into Europe, Catherine into the Crimea, the Romanovs into the cellar where they were shot. It crosses the trenches of the First World War into the chaos of 1917, into the famines and purges of Stalin's revolution from above, into the long, strange Cold War, and out the other side into the wild capitalism of the 1990s and the resentful resurgence of the present.

Along the way, characters who deserve more than a paragraph will get a chapter, and centuries that deserve only a few pages will get only a few pages. There will be saints and serial killers, poets and police chiefs, peasants who never learned to read and aristocrats who wrote in French because they could barely speak Russian. There will be moments of extraordinary courage and moments of bottomless cruelty, often in the same room on the same afternoon.

Somewhere on the south bank of the Dnieper, more than a thousand years ago, a small group of men decided to keep going. Everything that follows turned on that decision, and on the thousand decisions like it that came after.

The decision made on the south bank of the Dnieper did not arise from nothing. Before there was a Russia to refuse to end, there were rivers, and men who knew how to use them. The thousand years begin not with a saint or a tsar but with a boat shallow enough to be dragged across a watershed, and with crews willing to do the dragging. To find the first of the decisions that everything turned on, we have to go north, into the forests and lakes where the keels were cut and the long road south first opened.

Chapter 1
Rivers of the North: The Birth of Rus

The Varangian Question

The boats were long and shallow, built to be dragged. That is the detail to hold onto. When a Scandinavian crew came to the end of one river system and needed to reach another, they hauled the keel overland on rollers of cut log, sometimes for miles, until they found water deep enough to float them again. The whole northern half of Europe, in the ninth century, was navigable to anyone willing to row, portage, and fight.

The men who did this work were called Varangians in the east and Vikings in the west, and they were the same kind of men. They came down from the Baltic looking for silver, slaves, furs, wax, and honey, and they found a system of rivers that, with enough portaging, would carry them all the way to the Black Sea and Constantinople. The Volkhov led them to Lake Ilmen. From there they crossed to the headwaters of the Dnieper. The Dnieper carried them south through forest and then through open steppe to the Greeks. Another branch took them east to the Volga and the markets of the Caspian. Wherever they paused long enough to build a stockade, a town tended to grow up around them.

How much of the early Russian state these northerners actually founded, and how much they merely walked into, is the oldest argument in Russian historiography. The principal source is the Primary Chronicle, compiled in Kiev in the early twelfth century, which tells a famous story: the quarreling Slavic and Finnic tribes of the north, unable to govern themselves, sent across the sea to a people called the Rus and asked them to come and rule. Three brothers came: Rurik, Sineus, and Truvor. Rurik settled at Novgorod. His descendants would rule in the east for the next seven centuries. The story is too neat. It has the shape of a foundation myth, the kind a dynasty composes about itself after the fact. The brothers' names may be Norse, but two of them seem to be misreadings of Old Swedish phrases rather than people. Whether a real warlord named Rurik ever existed is something the sources cannot settle.

What is not in doubt is the archaeological record. At Staraya Ladoga, on the southern shore of the lake of the same name, Scandinavian artifacts begin appearing in the mid-eighth century: combs, brooches, weapons, runic graffiti. Further south at Gnezdovo, near Smolensk, excavators have opened hundreds of burials with a mixed population of Scandinavians and Slavs living in close proximity for generations. Arab silver dirhams, struck in Baghdad and Samarkand, pile up in hoards across the Russian plain in quantities that dwarf what was reaching western Europe at the same time. The Varangians were not raiders passing through. They were settling, marrying, trading, and within two or three generations becoming something else.

That something else is what historians call the Rus. The name itself is contested - probably from an Old Norse word for rowers, perhaps adopted by Finns to describe the strangers across the water, then passed on to the Slavs. By the tenth century, when Byzantine ambassadors recorded the names of Rus envoys, the men signing treaties had Norse names: Karl, Ingjald, Farulf. By the eleventh century, their grandsons were called Vladimir and Yaroslav and prayed in Slavonic. The conquerors had been absorbed by the conquered, or perhaps the two had simply fused into a third thing that was neither.

What mattered, in the end, was not where the founders came from but what they founded: a chain of fortified river-towns running north to south, ruled by a single warrior family, taxing the forests for furs and the rivers for transit, and selling everything they could collect to Constantinople.

Kiev: City on the Dnieper

The city stood on a bluff above the right bank of the Dnieper, where the river makes a wide bend and the steppe begins to open toward the south. From the heights you could see for miles in every direction: the river itself, the lower town spreading down toward the harbor, the green tongue of forest behind, and beyond the forest the flat horizon of the grass that ran all the way to the Caspian. It was a good place to watch for enemies and a good place to tax merchants. The Rus took it sometime in the late ninth century, and within a hundred years it had become the largest city in eastern Europe.

Kiev's wealth came from the river. Every spring, after the ice broke, fleets of dugout boats came down the Dnieper from the upriver tributaries, loaded with furs collected as tribute from the Slavic and Finnic tribes of the north. At Kiev the cargoes were transferred to larger vessels and the convoy assembled. The journey south to Constantinople was the most dangerous part of the year. Below the city the river narrowed into a series of rapids - the Greeks called them barrages, and the tenth-century emperor Constantine Porphyrogenitus left a description of each one by name, with notes on how the crews unloaded their cargo and dragged the boats over the rocks while armed men watched the banks for Pecheneg raiders.

If they made it past the rapids, the merchants reached the Black Sea and turned west along the coast to the imperial city. There they sold their furs, their honey, their wax, and their slaves, and bought silks, wine, glass, and gold. The treaties they signed with Byzantium - in 911, in 944 - laid out the terms with the precision of a guild charter: how many Rus merchants could enter the city at one time, where they would be lodged, what compensation was owed if one of them was killed in a brawl. The Greeks treated them as dangerous but useful trading partners. The Rus treated the Greeks as the source of nearly everything worth having.

The princes who ruled in Kiev in those decades were warriors first and administrators second. Oleg, who according to tradition moved the seat south from Novgorod around 882, was remembered for nailing his shield to the gates of Constantinople. Igor was killed by the Drevlians, a Slavic tribe northwest of Kiev, when he tried to extract a second tribute from them in a single year. His widow Olga avenged him with a thoroughness that the chroniclers half-admired and half-shuddered to record: she burned their capital, killed their elders, and reduced the survivors to ordinary tributaries. Then she went to Constantinople, was baptized, and came home a Christian. Her son Svyatoslav, who refused the new faith and went on campaigning until he was killed by Pechenegs on his way back from the Balkans, had his skull made into a drinking cup by the khan who killed him.

This was the dynasty Vladimir inherited in 980. Three generations in, the Rus rulers still lived largely on horseback. They wintered in Kiev and spent the rest of the year touring their territory, taking tribute, settling disputes, and fighting whichever of their cousins had recently rebelled. The court spoke Slavic now, but the structures of authority were still those of a warband: the prince surrounded by his druzhina, the retinue of mounted retainers who ate at his table and rode at his stirrup, paid in plunder and in shares of the tribute.

What Kiev did not yet have was anything resembling a state ideology. There was no shared religion that bound the prince to his subjects, or his subjects to one another. The Slavs worshipped a scattered pantheon - Perun the thunderer, Veles the lord of cattle and the underworld, Mokosh the spinner of fates - and the Varangians had brought their own. Vladimir tried, early in his reign, to standardize the old religion. He set up wooden idols on a hill above the city, with Perun at their head, and ordered sacrifices made there. It did not take. Within a decade he was looking for something else.

Vladimir's Choice and the Coming of Christianity

The Primary Chronicle gives the story in the form of a comedy. Envoys arrived in Kiev from the four great monotheisms of the medieval world, each pressing his own faith. The Volga Bulgars came first and offered Islam. Vladimir listened politely and then asked about the prohibition on wine. When they confirmed it, he replied that drinking was the joy of the Rus and they could not live without it, and sent them home. The Jews of Khazaria came next and were dismissed when they admitted that their God had scattered them from their homeland - hardly a recommendation, in the view of a man looking for divine backing. Latin Christians from the German emperor were heard and rejected too, for reasons the chronicler does not make entirely clear. Only the Greeks impressed him.

So Vladimir sent his own envoys to investigate. They reported back from Constantinople with the line that every Russian schoolchild eventually learns: when they stood inside the great church of Hagia Sophia during the liturgy, they did not know whether they were on earth or in heaven. That was the kingdom Vladimir bought into in 988.

The story is too tidy, like most of what the Chronicle gives us about the early princes, and the real calculation behind the conversion was almost certainly diplomatic. Vladimir had been negotiating with the Byzantine emperor Basil II, who needed military help against an internal revolt. The price for sending six thousand Rus troops was the hand of Basil's sister Anna - a porphyrogenita, born in the imperial palace, a marriage prize never before granted to a barbarian ruler. The condition was that Vladimir accept Christianity. He accepted. He took Anna as his wife, sent the troops, and returned to Kiev to baptize his people.

The baptism itself, as the chroniclers describe it, took place in the Dnieper. Vladimir ordered the citizens of Kiev to wade into the river on a chosen morning, and the priests who had come with Anna's retinue performed the rite from the bank. The old idols were thrown down. Perun was dragged through the streets behind horses, beaten with sticks by men assigned to the task, and finally tipped into the river. Some accounts say the crowds wept as the god floated downstream. Whether they wept for him or simply at the strangeness of what was happening, the chronicler does not say.

Conversion from the top was not unusual in early medieval Europe, and it rarely meant what the missionaries hoped. In the countryside, the old gods went on being worshipped under new names. Perun's attributes attached themselves to the prophet Elijah, who drove a thunder-chariot across the sky. Mokosh became confused with the Virgin. The peasant calendar of fertility rites and seasonal festivals absorbed the church year without fully surrendering to it. Centuries later, Russian priests were still complaining about villagers who left offerings at sacred springs and tied ribbons to particular trees. What Vladimir's baptism actually changed, immediately, was the apparatus of the state.

It changed it considerably. A bishop arrived from Constantinople. A metropolitan see was established, subordinate to the patriarch in the imperial city. Churches went up in Kiev - the Church of the Tithes was the first major stone building, financed by a tenth of the prince's revenue, as its name advertised. With the church came writing, in the Slavonic script developed a century earlier by the missionaries Cyril and Methodius for use among the Slavs of Moravia. Greek liturgical books were translated. A clerical class began to form, drawn at first from Byzantine and Bulgarian recruits and gradually from native Rus.

The choice of eastern Christianity rather than western had consequences nobody in 988 could have foreseen. Latin Christianity, with its insistence on the Roman liturgy and the Roman language, would tie its converts into the cultural world of western Europe - eventually into universities, scholastic theology, and the long quarrels of medieval kings and popes. Eastern Christianity gave its converts the Slavonic liturgy and the model of the Christian emperor as God's regent on earth. It was a more self-contained tradition, less hungry for outside contact, and when

Constantinople fell to the Turks four and a half centuries later, the Russian church would find itself almost alone in the world. The seed of that long isolation was planted on the bank of the Dnieper in the summer of 988.

Vladimir lived another twenty-seven years. He built churches, supported the new clergy, and was eventually canonized for his trouble. When he died in 1015, he left twelve sons by various wives and no settled rule of succession. What followed was the kind of fight that the dynasty would have many more times.

Yaroslav the Wise and the Russian Truth

Yaroslav was in Novgorod when news came that his father was dead. He had been governing the northern city as vice-regent for several years, and he had quarreled with Vladimir over tribute - he had refused to send Kiev its annual share, and the two had been on the edge of open war when the old prince's death made the question moot.

His brother Svyatopolk moved first. Within months of Vladimir's funeral, three of Yaroslav's brothers were dead. Boris and Gleb, the youngest, were murdered by men sent from Kiev; their deaths, which they were said to have accepted without resistance, would later make them the first saints of the Russian church. A third brother, Svyatoslav, was hunted down as he tried to flee to Hungary. The chronicler called Svyatopolk the Accursed and the name stuck. Yaroslav came south with a mixed force of Novgorodians and Varangian mercenaries. He took Kiev in 1016, lost it again to Svyatopolk in 1018 when his brother returned with Polish help, and finally won it back for good in 1019. Even then he did not rule the whole inheritance. His brother Mstislav, ruling in Tmutarakan on the Black Sea coast, defeated him in battle in 1024, and the two settled into an uneasy division of the realm along the Dnieper. Only when Mstislav died in 1036 did Yaroslav become sole ruler of the Rus.

He held that position for the next eighteen years, and during those years Kiev became something close to what the chroniclers wanted it to be. The Pechenegs, the nomadic raiders who had harried the city for generations, were beaten so badly outside its walls in 1036 that they ceased to be a serious threat. Yaroslav celebrated the victory by building, on the site of the battle, a stone cathedral modeled on Hagia Sophia in Constantinople - the Cathedral of St. Sophia, which still stands. Its interior was covered in mosaics and frescoes done by Greek craftsmen, with portraits of Yaroslav's own family in the western gallery. A few hundred yards away he raised the Golden Gate, the ceremonial entrance to the city, copied in name and concept from the gate of the imperial capital.

What Yaroslav wanted, and what his court increasingly produced, was a Kievan culture that could claim parity with Byzantium. He collected books. He had Greek texts translated into Slavonic. He founded schools attached to the cathedral and the major monasteries. The Monastery of the Caves, established outside the city in his reign, would become the most important religious house in the eastern Slavic world and the cradle of the chronicle tradition that gives us most of what we know about him.

He also commissioned, or at least patronized, the first written compilation of Rus law - the Russkaya Pravda, the Russian Truth. It is a short document by the standards of medieval law codes, perhaps thirty or forty articles in its earliest form, and it deals largely with the kinds of disputes that actually arose: theft, assault, debt, the murder of one man by another and the compensation owed to his kin. The fines are calibrated by rank. A free man's life is worth so many grivnas of silver; a prince's retainer's life is worth more; a slave's life is worth less. The blood feud is permitted within limits, then increasingly replaced by payment. The Russkaya Pravda was not Roman law and made no pretense of being so. It was Scandinavian and Slavic custom written down, with a Christian gloss.

Yaroslav's diplomatic reach matched his cultural ambition. His daughters married kings of France, Norway, and Hungary; his sons married into the imperial families of Byzantium and Germany. The court at Kiev was not a provincial place. It received envoys from Rome and Constantinople and sent its own people across half of Europe. When he died in 1054, Yaroslav was buried in St. Sophia. His tomb, a marble sarcophagus probably brought from Cherson, is still there. He had divided his realm among his surviving sons before his death and left them, the chronicler reports, with instructions to love one another. It did not work.

Fragmentation and the Princes' Wars

The system Yaroslav left behind was meant to keep the dynasty together. It did the opposite.

The principle was rotation by seniority. The eldest brother got Kiev. The next-eldest got Chernigov. The next got Pereyaslavl. And so down the list of cities, each son holding a throne that corresponded to his place in the family hierarchy. When one of them died, everyone moved up a step: the prince of Chernigov took Kiev, the prince of Pereyaslavl took Chernigov, and so on. The arrangement assumed that the dynasty would remain a single family with a single sense of itself, and that brothers would accept the deaths of brothers as occasions for orderly promotion rather than for seizing whatever city happened to be within reach. It worked for one generation, more or less. Yaroslav's three eldest sons - Izyaslav, Svyatoslav, and Vsevolod - ruled together for nearly twenty years, sometimes called the triumvirate by modern historians, and during that time they reissued the Russkaya Pravda with additions and beat back a serious nomadic invasion. Then Svyatoslav, the middle brother, took Kiev for himself in 1073 by driving Izyaslav out. The system never recovered.

By the early twelfth century there were more princes than there were major thrones, and the genealogical bookkeeping required to determine who outranked whom had become impossibly tangled. A cousin from a senior branch of the family might be younger than a cousin from a junior branch; a prince who had been bypassed for Kiev in one generation might claim that his sons were therefore permanently excluded too, while his nephews insisted on the opposite. The cities themselves grew tired of being passed from prince to prince every few years and began to assert their own preferences. Novgorod, in particular, increasingly chose its own rulers and dismissed them when displeased.

The Pechenegs were gone, but the steppe was not empty. A new nomadic people, the Polovtsy - the Cumans to western writers - had moved into the grass south of Kiev by the mid-eleventh century. They were better organized than the Pechenegs and harder to break. They raided the southern principalities every few years and sometimes hired themselves out to one prince against another. By the twelfth century, civil wars among the Rurikids regularly included Polovtsian auxiliaries on both sides.

The economy of the river-trade was changing too. The Crusades opened new routes from western Europe to the eastern Mediterranean, bypassing the Dnieper. The Byzantine market for furs and slaves did not vanish, but it ceased to be the only game in the region. Cities further north and west - Novgorod with its Baltic connections, Vladimir and Suzdal in the forested northeast where new lands were being cleared and settled - grew at the expense of the old southern center.

In 1169 the prince of Vladimir-Suzdal, Andrei Bogolyubsky, sent an army south against Kiev. The city was sacked. It had been sacked before in dynastic quarrels, but this time the prince who took it declined to move there. He had no intention of leaving his northern capital for the old mother of cities on the Dnieper. He sent a junior relative to govern Kiev and went back to Vladimir.

That was the signal, if anyone was paying attention, that the center of gravity had shifted. The rivers that had carried the first Rus south to Constantinople still ran, and the boats still went down them every spring. But the men who mattered were already looking the other way, toward the forests of the upper Volga, where a different kind of Russia was being built among the pines.

The shift of gravity from Kiev to the northern forests would prove, in time, to have saved something and doomed something else. The princes who looked toward the upper Volga were building a different kind of Russia, one harder to reach by river and harder to see from Constantinople. They would need that distance sooner than they knew. The horsemen who would change everything were already crossing grass that no Rus chronicler had yet learned to name, and the rumor of them had not yet reached the rivers where the spring boats still went down each year.

Chapter 2
Under the Mongol Shadow

The Coming of Batu Khan

The first warning came in 1223, at a river called the Kalka, somewhere on the open grass north of the Sea of Azov. A combined force of Rus princes and their Polovtsian allies rode out to meet a strange new enemy who had appeared from beyond the Caspian. The Rus had heard rumors but knew almost nothing: who these horsemen were, where they came from, what god they served. They learned by being broken in a single afternoon. The princes who survived the field were laid under wooden planks, and the victors sat down on top of those planks to feast while the men beneath them suffocated. Then the horsemen turned their ponies east and disappeared as suddenly as they had come.

For thirteen years there was nothing. The princes went back to feuding with one another. Kiev quarreled with Vladimir. Chernigov quarreled with everyone. The lesson of the Kalka, if there was a lesson, faded into the long catalogue of bad years.

In 1236, Batu Khan, grandson of Genghis, crossed the Volga with an army authorized by the Great Khan Ögedei in distant Karakorum. With him rode Subutai, the old general who had been at the Kalka and remembered everything. The Mongols were not raiders. They had come to stay, or at least to make the country pay tribute forever, and they had a method.

The method began at Ryazan in the winter of 1237. The prince of Ryazan asked his neighbors for help. None came. Mongol envoys had already arrived demanding a tenth of everything - a tenth of the horses, a tenth of the men, a tenth of the women. The prince refused. The city held out for five days. When the walls came down, the chronicler wrote that there was no one left to weep for the dead.

Then Kolomna. Then Moscow, still a small wooden town on the Moskva. Then Vladimir, the grandest city in the northeast, where Grand Prince Yuri's wife and sons took refuge in the cathedral and were burned alive when the Mongols set the roof on fire. Yuri himself was killed on the Sit River in March 1238. The chronicler of Novgorod, which the Mongols spared because the spring thaw turned the roads to swamp, listed fourteen cities sacked in a single winter campaign and then stopped counting.

The southern cities had two more years. In December 1240, after a siege whose noise was said to drown out conversation inside the city, Kiev fell. The mother of Rus cities, the seat of Vladimir who had baptized the Slavs, was leveled. A papal envoy named John of Plano Carpini passed through five years later and reported that the bones of the dead still lay in heaps in the fields, and that the surviving population had shrunk to a few hundred souls huddling in the ruins.

Batu did not press on into central Europe for long. In 1241 his armies tore through Poland and Hungary, but the death of Ögedei in Karakorum pulled him back. He settled instead on the lower Volga, where he built a new capital called Sarai - a city of tents that grew into a city of brick, with mosques and bathhouses and a market that connected China to the Mediterranean. From Sarai he ruled what came to be known as the Golden Horde. And from Sarai, for the next two and a half centuries, the princes of Rus would receive their orders.

In the winter of 1237–38, Batu Khan's armies swept across frozen rivers into the heart of Rus, destroying city after city. The devastation reshaped the political geography of eastern Europe for generations.

Yoke or Partnership? Living Under the Horde

The Russian word for what came next is *igo*, the yoke. It is a heavy word, and it carries the verdict of later centuries: that Russia was crushed, humiliated, cut off from Europe, dragged into Asiatic darkness. For a long time this was the only version of the story anyone told. More recent historians have argued the picture is more complicated - that what looks from one angle like a yoke looks from another like a working arrangement between conquerors who wanted taxes and a conquered people who wanted to be left alone. Both versions contain truth, and neither contains all of it.

The mechanics were straightforward. The Mongols did not occupy the Russian forests. They did not garrison the cities or settle the land. What they wanted was tribute, and to get it they needed to know how many people there were. So in the 1250s, Mongol officials called *baskaks* moved through the principalities with scribes and abacuses, counting households. Every tenth man owed military service. Every household owed a tax in silver. The princes were left in place, but each had to travel to Sarai - and sometimes onward to Karakorum, a journey of months - to receive a *yarlyk*, a patent of authority, from the khan personally. Without the yarlyk a prince was nothing. With it he ruled by Mongol license.

The journey to Sarai was a humiliation by design. Princes passed between two fires for ritual purification. They knelt. They presented gifts. Some were murdered there on suspicion of disloyalty, including Grand Prince Mikhail of Chernigov, who refused to bow to a Mongol idol and was beaten to death in 1246. Others returned home loaded with honors and the right to collect taxes from their rivals. That last detail mattered. The Mongols did not unify the Rus principalities; they played them against each other. A prince who carried tales of his neighbor's disloyalty to Sarai might come home with the khan's permission to sack that neighbor's town. Mongol detachments rode along on these expeditions when invited. The yoke, in practice, was a network of grudges that the khans tended carefully.

What did Russia absorb from its overlords? The arguments have run for two hundred years. Some borrowings are uncontested: the postal relay system, the census, the customs of taxation, certain military formations, a vocabulary of money and horses and administration that still sits in modern Russian - words for treasury, for customs, for caravan, for whip. Some borrowings are stranger. The autocratic style of later Russian rulers, the habit of treating subjects as property of the throne, the practice of prostration before a sovereign - all of these have been traced, by some historians, to the Mongol model. Others reply that Byzantium offered the same examples and Russia would have found its way to autocracy on its own. The argument cannot be settled.

The Orthodox Church, meanwhile, did unexpectedly well. The Mongols were religiously tolerant, in the manner of empires that have many gods to keep track of and no patience for theology. They exempted Russian clergy from taxes and from military service, and they protected church lands. In the wreckage of the cities, the monasteries grew. Monks pushed north into forests that had never been cleared, founded new houses, copied old manuscripts. While the secular princes shuttled back and forth to Sarai with bags of silver, the abbots stayed home and prayed, and quietly accumulated land.

For ordinary people - the peasants who paid the tax and the townsmen who watched the *baskaks* ride through - the yoke was neither romantic nor metaphorical. It was a man at the door with a tally stick. What had been destroyed could not be replaced. The skilled glass and enamel workers of Kievan Rus were gone, killed in the sacks or carried off to Sarai. Stone churches stopped being built for half a century. The country grew quieter, poorer, more inward. When it began to recover, it recovered in a different shape.

Alexander Nevsky and the Choice of East over West

While the southern cities burned, Novgorod kept its republican council, its trade with the Baltic, and its young prince, Alexander Yaroslavich. He was about twenty in 1240, the year Kiev fell, and that summer the Swedes came up the Neva River intending to take advantage of the chaos. Alexander met them at the river's mouth with a small force of Novgorodian troops and his own druzhina, and beat them decisively. The victory gave him his surname: Nevsky, of the Neva.

Two years later, in April 1242, he faced a more serious enemy. The Teutonic Knights, a German crusading order that had been pushing east through the Baltic for decades, advanced on Novgorod across the frozen surface of Lake Peipus. The battle that followed has been mythologized into something almost cinematic - the ice cracking under the weight of the armored knights, the Russian foot soldiers waiting in the shallows - and the cinematic version owes a great deal to Sergei Eisenstein's 1938 film. The historical battle was smaller and less spectacular. But Alexander won it, and he stopped the Catholic advance into Orthodox lands.

Then he made a different kind of choice. He went to Sarai and bowed to the khan.

The contrast was deliberate, and it defined the rest of his career. To the west, where the popes were promising military aid in exchange for conversion to Rome, Alexander said no. To the east, where the Mongols demanded tribute and submission but did not care what god the Russians prayed to, he said yes. He traveled to Sarai repeatedly. In 1252 the khan made him Grand Prince of Vladimir. When Novgorod resisted the Mongol census in 1257, it was Alexander himself who arrived with Mongol officials and forced the city to submit, putting out the eyes of the ringleaders, including, according to one account, his own son's supporters.

This is the part of the story that does not fit well in the heroic version. Alexander Nevsky was canonized by the Orthodox Church and became, in later centuries, a symbol of Russian resistance to foreign domination. Stalin awarded a military order in his name. But the actual Alexander spent more of his life enforcing Mongol authority than fighting it. He calculated that the Catholic West, with its crusades and its demand for spiritual surrender, was the greater threat. The Mongols took silver and left the icons alone. The Germans wanted the soul.

Whether he was right is a question Russians have been arguing about ever since. The nineteenth-century Westernizers thought he had set Russia on a backward path, cut off from the intellectual currents of Europe. The Slavophiles thought he had saved Russian Orthodoxy from absorption by a foreign church. Both sides were arguing about their own century as much as his.

Alexander died in 1263 on the way back from yet another journey to Sarai. He was forty-two. The Mongols had not killed him; the road had. He was buried at Vladimir, and the monk who wrote his life called him the sun of the Russian land. Outside the monastery walls, the tribute collectors went on with their work.

The Rise of Moscow

In 1147 Moscow appears in the chronicles for the first time, as a place where one prince invited another to come and dine. It was a small wooden settlement on a bluff above a river, useful mainly because several trade routes happened to meet there. A hundred years later the Mongols burned it down along with everything else. By any reasonable forecast in 1240, Moscow's future was to be a minor town in the shadow of Vladimir or Tver.

What changed was a combination of geography, luck, and a series of princes who were very good at a particular kind of politics. Moscow sat in the middle of the forest belt, far enough from the steppe that Mongol raiding parties had to make an effort to reach it, but close enough to the river network that goods and refugees flowed through it. As the southern lands emptied out - peasants fleeing the tribute collectors, monks fleeing the ruins - many of them drifted north into the territory the Muscovite princes controlled. Population was wealth in medieval Russia, and Moscow's population grew.

Luck came in the form of long-lived princes. The Muscovite line, descended from Alexander Nevsky's youngest son Daniel, had a habit of producing competent men who lived into their fifties and passed the throne to grown sons in orderly succession. The rival house of Tver, which had a stronger claim to seniority and for most of the early fourteenth century looked like the obvious leader of northeastern Rus, was repeatedly disrupted by feuds, executions at Sarai, and unlucky deaths.

The politics began in earnest with Ivan I, who took the Moscow throne in 1325 and earned the nickname Kalita - Moneybag. The name was literal. Ivan walked around with a purse on his belt from which, the chroniclers said, he gave alms to the poor. He also collected taxes for the Mongols, and he did it with such efficiency that the khan gave him the right to collect on behalf of all the Russian principalities. Whoever held the tax-farming contract for the Horde sat at the financial center of Russia. Some of the silver, inevitably, stayed in Moscow.

Ivan used the money to buy land. He bought villages from impoverished neighbors, monasteries, even other princes. He lent silver to lords who could not pay their tribute and foreclosed when they defaulted. He arranged marriages that brought territory with them. By the time he died in 1340, Moscow had quietly absorbed a ring of smaller principalities around itself, almost without anyone noticing how it had happened. He also persuaded the metropolitan of the Russian Church, Peter, to move his residence from Vladimir to Moscow. When Peter died there, his successor stayed. From the 1320s onward, the spiritual capital of Orthodox Rus was wherever the metropolitan happened to be, and the metropolitan was in Moscow. Pilgrims came. So did money. So did legitimacy.

None of this would have been possible without the Horde's blessing, and Ivan Kalita was careful to keep that blessing. When Tver rose in revolt against the Mongols in 1327, killing the khan's envoy and his retinue, it was Ivan who led the Mongol punitive expedition against his Russian rival. Tver was burned. Its prince was killed at Sarai a few years later. The grand princely title, which Tver had held, passed to Moscow.

This was a brutal kind of statecraft, and it does not produce heroes. Ivan Kalita was not loved by the chroniclers in the way Alexander Nevsky was loved. He was an accountant with a sword. But by the end of his reign, Moscow had stopped being one of several candidates for leadership of the Russian lands and become the obvious one.

Kulikovo and the Cracking of the Yoke

By the 1370s the Golden Horde was no longer the unified machine that had crossed the Volga with Batu. A succession of weak khans and palace coups - more than twenty rulers in twenty years, in some periods - had cracked the central authority. Power in Sarai had drifted into the hands of a general named Mamai, a man of military talent but no Genghisid blood, which meant he could rule in someone else's name but never legitimately wear the title himself.

In Moscow the grand prince was Dmitry Ivanovich, Ivan Kalita's grandson, then in his twenties. He had grown up in a court that still sent tribute to Sarai but had begun, quietly, to wonder whether it had to. He stopped some payments. He fortified the Kremlin in white stone, the first stone walls Moscow had ever had. In 1378 he beat a Mongol detachment at the Vozha River - a small engagement, but the first time a Russian army had won an open-field battle against the Horde since the Kalka a century and a half earlier.

Mamai understood that this could not stand. In the summer of 1380 he assembled a large army, including Genoese mercenaries from the Crimean trading posts, and arranged an alliance with the Grand Duke of Lithuania, Jogaila, who was to march east and join him. Dmitry, knowing what was coming, gathered men from across the Russian principalities. Not all of them came - Tver did not, and Novgorod hesitated - but more came than had ever rallied to a Russian banner before.

The two armies met on September 8, 1380, on a field called Kulikovo - the Field of Snipes - near the headwaters of the Don. Dmitry, according to the chronicles, exchanged armor with one of his boyars and fought in the front ranks as a common warrior. He was found after the battle unconscious under a tree, alive but badly bruised. The fighting lasted most of a day. A Russian reserve hidden in a wood charged at the decisive moment and broke the Mongol line. Mamai fled. Jogaila, hearing of the defeat while still on the march, turned around and went home.

Dmitry returned to Moscow as Dmitry Donskoy, of the Don. The victory was celebrated as deliverance. Monks wrote of it as a sign that God had not abandoned the Russian land. For the first time in a hundred and forty years, the khan's army had been beaten in the open by Russians who had ridden out specifically to fight it.

It did not end the yoke. Two years later a new khan, Tokhtamysh, who had restored some unity to the Horde, marched on Moscow while Dmitry was away gathering troops. He took the city by deceit, promising mercy if the gates were opened, and then sacked it. Twenty-four thousand people are said to have been killed. Dmitry came back to ruins and resumed paying tribute.

But something had changed that could not be unchanged. Kulikovo had shown that the Mongols could be beaten. The tribute continued, the yarlyks were still issued at Sarai, the humiliations went on for another century. The fear, though, was no longer absolute. A Russian who had been a boy at Kulikovo, telling the story to his grandchildren in the 1440s, knew that the men on the horses from the east were men, and that men could die in the long grass by a river.

The boy at Kulikovo who became a grandfather telling the story in the 1440s lived to see his grandsons inherit something his own father could not have imagined: the idea that the men from the steppe were beatable, and that the tribute, however long it lasted, would not last forever. The fear had loosened. What rose in its place, slowly, in the principality that had learned to collect the khan's taxes most efficiently of all, was a different kind of confidence. Moscow had been the obedient servant of Sarai. It was beginning, quietly, to become something else.

Chapter 3
The Third Rome: Muscovy Ascendant

Ivan III and the Gathering of the Lands

In the autumn of 1480, two armies stood on opposite banks of the Ugra River, about a hundred and fifty miles southwest of Moscow, and watched each other. On one side was Khan Akhmat of the Great Horde, expecting tribute. On the other was Ivan III, Grand Prince of Moscow, who had refused to send it. Neither commander wanted to attack across the water. The autumn dragged on. The river began to freeze. In November, Akhmat turned his army around and went home.

That was how Mongol rule over Moscow ended - not with a battle but with a man who refused to bow, and a khan who could no longer compel him.

Ivan had come to the throne in 1462 at the age of twenty-two. He inherited a principality that had been a tributary of the Horde for more than two centuries and that shared the central Russian plain with a dozen rival princes, some of them his own cousins, and with two great independent powers to the north and west: the merchant republic of Novgorod and the Grand Duchy of Lithuania. By the time he died in 1505, almost all of it was his. The chroniclers called the process the gathering of the lands, as though Moscow were simply collecting what had always belonged to it. The reality was harder, slower, and bloodier.

Novgorod was the great prize. It was the richest city in the Russian north, controlling the fur trade with the Baltic and Scandinavia, governed by an assembly of free citizens that traced its origins to the Viking age. Its merchants traded with Hanseatic towns, read Latin, and looked west. In 1471 a faction in Novgorod attempted to place the city under the protection of Catholic Lithuania. Ivan marched. He defeated the Novgorodian army at the Shelon River and forced the city to acknowledge his sovereignty. Seven years later, in 1478, he came back and finished the work. He dissolved the assembly. He carried off the great bell that had summoned citizens to debate. He deported hundreds of leading families and resettled their lands with men loyal to Moscow. The merchant republic ceased to exist.

With Novgorod gone, the smaller principalities had little choice. Tver, Moscow's old rival, was annexed in 1485 after its prince fled to Lithuania. Vyatka followed in 1489. Ryazan and Pskov remained nominally independent but lived under Muscovite shadow. Ivan also pushed west into territories held by Lithuania, picking off border towns one at a time, and he opened diplomatic correspondence with the Holy Roman Emperor, the Ottoman Sultan, and the Pope. None of his predecessors had behaved like the ruler of a serious state. Ivan did.

The instruments of his rule were sharper than anything Moscow had used before. In 1497 he promulgated the Sudebnik, the first standardized law code for the whole of his territory. It set out penalties, court procedures, and the duties of officials. It also, in a single short article, restricted the days on which a peasant could legally leave his lord's land to a two-week window around St. George's Day in November. That clause, scarcely noticed at the time, would prove to be one of the most consequential lines of law in Russian history.

Foreign visitors began to describe him as something closer to an emperor than a prince. He had started to use the title *gosudar* - sovereign - and on his official seals he placed the double-headed eagle. The eagle, like much else in his court, came from Constantinople. Or rather, from what had been Constantinople, because by then Constantinople was something else.

Marriage to Byzantium

The proposal came from Rome. In 1469 a Greek cardinal named Bessarion, who had spent his life trying to reunite the Latin and Orthodox churches, suggested that the niece of the last Byzantine Emperor might make a suitable bride for the widower Grand Prince of Moscow. Her name was Zoe Palaiologina. She had been raised in Italy as a Catholic ward of the Pope after her family fled the fall of the city. She was about fifteen.

The Pope had his own reasons for liking the match. He hoped Zoe might draw Moscow into a Catholic alliance against the Turks, or at least open the door to church union. Ivan had different reasons. He was a widower with one son, but the political weight of the marriage mattered more than the dynasty. To marry a Palaiologina was to attach himself, however thinly, to the imperial line of Constantine. It was a claim, written in flesh.

Negotiations took three years. In 1472 Zoe traveled overland from Rome through Germany and the Baltic and arrived in Moscow in November. Somewhere along the way she stopped being Zoe and became Sophia. She arrived as an Orthodox woman, or at least presented herself as one; the papal legate who accompanied her was politely shunted aside, his processional cross hidden as the party entered the city. The wedding took place in a wooden cathedral on the Kremlin hill. The papal mission went home with nothing.

What Moscow got was harder to measure. Sophia brought a retinue of Greek scholars and Italian craftsmen, books, ceremonial habits, and the memory of a court that had once ruled from the Bosphorus. She brought, by tradition though not by certainty, the double-headed eagle that would become the emblem of the Russian state. She brought, above all, the idea that her husband was not merely the prince of a forest principality but the heir, by marriage, of Caesar.

Foreign ambassadors noticed a change in Ivan's court after her arrival. Ceremonial became more elaborate. Access to the sovereign was restricted. Boyars who had once spoken to the prince as kinsmen now approached him in silence and bowed lower. Sophia herself was reported to have urged her husband to throw off the last vestiges of Mongol subordination and to behave like the emperor she believed he was. The chronicles are not fond of her - she was a foreigner, a woman, and she meddled - but they record her presence at the major decisions of the reign.

She bore Ivan twelve children. Her eldest son, Vasily, would eventually succeed his father after a long and ugly succession struggle against the children of Ivan's first marriage. Through Vasily and his son Ivan IV, Byzantine blood entered the line of Moscow's rulers and stayed there until the end of the dynasty in 1598. Whether any of this would have mattered without what was happening in the monasteries is another question. A marriage by itself does not make an empire. It takes a story, and the story was being written elsewhere, in the cells of monks who had never seen Constantinople and never would.

The Idea of the Third Rome

The first Rome had fallen to barbarians. The second Rome, Constantinople, had fallen to the Turks in 1453, an event that struck Orthodox Christians the way the death of a parent strikes a grown child: long expected and still devastating. For a thousand years the Byzantine Emperor had been the temporal head of Orthodox Christendom, the figure under whose authority the patriarchs gathered and the liturgy was celebrated. Now he was dead in the streets and the Hagia Sophia was a mosque.

Russian churchmen had been preparing for this loss longer than they knew. In 1439 the Byzantine delegation at the Council of Florence had agreed to submit to Rome in exchange for Western military aid against the Turks. The aid never came; the union was repudiated by most of the Orthodox world; but in Moscow it was taken as proof that Constantinople had betrayed the faith. When the city fell fourteen years later, many in Russia read the fall as God's judgment on apostasy. The Greeks had sold their birthright. The torch had to pass somewhere else.

It passed, according to a monk named Philotheos of the Eleazarov monastery in Pskov, to Moscow. Sometime in the early sixteenth century - the dating is uncertain - Philotheos wrote a letter to the Grand Prince Vasily III, Ivan's son, that contained the sentences that would define an idea for the next four hundred years. Two Romes had fallen. A third stood. A fourth there would not be.

The doctrine of the Third Rome was, at its origin, a piece of monastic correspondence, not a political program. Philotheos was concerned with the purity of the faith and the responsibility of the Orthodox ruler to defend it. He was not proposing imperial expansion or military conquest. But the idea, once articulated, took on a life Philotheos could not have predicted. If Moscow was the last refuge of true Christianity, then her ruler was not merely a prince among princes. He was the protector of the faith on earth. He answered to no other Christian sovereign.

The title *tsar*, a Slavic rendering of Caesar, had been used loosely before for the Mongol khans and occasionally for the Byzantine emperors. Ivan III began to use it of himself. His grandson Ivan IV would make it official at his coronation in 1547. By then the chain of associations was complete: Caesar to Constantine to Moscow, with the double-headed eagle as its sign and the cross of Saint Andrew as its protection.

How much ordinary Russians believed of all this is a fair question. The peasant in a Vladimir village did not know who Philotheos was and would have understood little of his theology. The merchants of Novgorod, those who survived, would have laughed bitterly. But in the chancelleries of the Kremlin and in the cells of the great monasteries, the idea took hold and grew. It gave Moscow a vocabulary for what she was becoming. It supplied a justification for power that could be stated in the language of the church rather than the language of conquest. And it bound the Russian state to the Orthodox faith in a way that no later upheaval - not Peter's westernization, not Bolshevik atheism, not the chaos of the 1990s - has entirely undone.

The Kremlin Rises

The walls Ivan inherited were made of white limestone, more than a century old, cracked in places, patched with timber where the stone had failed. The cathedrals inside were small wooden buildings that had been rebuilt many times after fires. It was a serviceable fortress for a serviceable principality. It was not the seat of an empire.

Ivan brought in Italians. The first was Aristotele Fioravanti of Bologna, a military engineer and architect who had worked for the Sforza in Milan and for the King of Hungary. He arrived in Moscow in 1475 and was given a single commission: rebuild the Cathedral of the Dormition, the church in which the Metropolitan of Moscow was enthroned, after the previous attempt had collapsed during construction. Fioravanti went to Vladimir to study the old Russian churches, then designed a building that combined Russian forms - five domes, a cross-in-square plan, the white stone walls - with Italian engineering. The cathedral he finished in 1479 is still standing.

More Italians followed. Marco Ruffo and Pietro Antonio Solari built the new red brick walls of the Kremlin between 1485 and 1495, replacing the limestone with brick whose distinctive M-shaped battlements echoed the Sforza castle in Milan. They built the great towers - the Spasskaya, the Nikolskaya, the Borovitskaya - whose silhouettes still define the skyline above the Moskva River. They built the Palace of Facets, the audience hall whose diamond-cut stone facade gave it its name, where the tsars would receive ambassadors for the next two centuries.

The result was strange and beautiful. Inside the walls, Russian masters built churches in the old style: the Cathedral of the Annunciation, the small private chapel of the grand princes, and later the Cathedral of the Archangel, where the rulers of Moscow would be buried. Outside, the walls were Lombard. The whole was unmistakably neither Italian nor Russian but something new - a fortress-city that announced itself as the seat of a power drawing on both the Byzantine east and the Latin west without belonging to either. Foreigners who visited in the late fifteenth and sixteenth centuries described being struck by the contrast between the splendor of the Kremlin and the wooden chaos of the city around it. Moscow proper was still a town of log houses, muddy streets, and constant fires. But the citadel on the hill - white cathedrals, gold domes, red walls, the river at its foot - looked like the capital of a serious empire. Which was the point.

Ivan understood what his Italians had given him. He had not just rebuilt a fortress. He had built a stage.

Serfdom and the Binding of the Peasant

The peasant in the Russian forest belt in 1450 was, by the standards of his Polish or German contemporary, a relatively free man. He held land from a lord in exchange for rent and labor, but he could in principle pack up his household and move to another lord's estate if the terms were better, or to the wild lands of the south and east if he wanted no lord at all. The Russian frontier was vast, sparsely populated, and forgiving of those who could survive its winters. Labor was scarce. Lords competed for tenants by offering favorable terms.

This system was already under strain when Ivan came to the throne. As Moscow consolidated its grip on the central Russian lands, it created a new class of servitor: the *pomeshchik*, a cavalryman granted an estate in return for military service. The pomeshchik did not own his land outright. He held it from the sovereign as long as he served. To make the grant worth anything, the estate had to produce income, which meant it had to have peasants on it to work the soil. If those peasants could leave whenever they wished, the pomeshchik could not pay for his horse and armor, and the army Ivan was building would not exist.

The solution emerged piece by piece, not as a single decree. The Sudebnik of 1497 was the first move. It did not abolish the peasant's right to leave. It simply restricted that right to a two-week window once a year, around St. George's Day in late November, after the harvest was in and the accounts could be settled. The peasant who wished to move had to pay an exit fee and had to be free of debt to his lord. In practice he was almost never free of debt, because lords advanced grain, seed, and tools at terms that bound the tenant tighter with each passing season.

Subsequent rulers tightened the screws. The St. George's Day window was suspended in the late sixteenth century, first as a temporary measure during years of famine and war, then permanently. Time limits on the recovery of runaway peasants were extended, and eventually abolished. By the Ulozhenie of 1649, more than a century after Ivan's death, the peasant was legally bound to the land and could be sold with it. What had begun under Ivan as a regulation of mobility had become serfdom in its full and ugly maturity.

The binding of the Russian peasant is one of the most consequential developments in the country's history and one of the easiest to misread. It was not the product of a single tyrant's cruelty. It was the slow accumulation of practical decisions made by rulers who needed soldiers, soldiers who needed estates, estates that needed workers, and a state that needed taxes. Each decision answered an immediate problem. The cumulative result was a society in which the great majority of the population - by the eighteenth century, perhaps four out of five Russians - had been reduced to a condition closer to slavery than to peasantry as the term was understood in the West.

The same decades in which the Kremlin acquired its red walls and its imperial vocabulary, in which Moscow declared herself the Third Rome and the heir of Caesar, were the decades in which the peasant on whom all of it depended lost the right to walk away. The empire rose. The man in the village stayed where he was put.

Outside the walls, the snow fell on log houses where families bedded down with their animals for warmth. Inside the walls, the candles burned in the Cathedral of the Dormition, and a Greek princess from Rome watched her husband hold court like an emperor.

Inside the Kremlin walls the candles burned and the Greek princess watched her husband perform an emperor's role. Outside the walls the peasant stayed where he was put. The arrangement worked because the man at its center believed in it and because the men around him agreed, for their own reasons, to let him believe. What happened when the man at the center was a child, watched by boyars who did not bother to hide their contempt, was a question Muscovy had not yet had to answer. It was about to.

Chapter 4
Ivan the Terrible and the Forge of Autocracy

The Boy Tsar

He was three when his father died, eight when his mother was buried, and by most accounts she had been poisoned. The boy who would become Ivan IV grew up in the Kremlin as a kind of orphan-prince, watched but not protected, surrounded by boyars who bowed to him in public and ignored him in private. He later remembered being made to wait for food. He remembered grandees lounging on his father's bed in his presence, their boots on the furniture, addressing him as if he were a servant's child.

The court he inherited in 1533 was a court of factions. The great families - the Shuiskys, the Belskys, the Glinskys - fought for control of the regency and, through it, control of Muscovy itself. They poisoned each other, arrested each other, exiled each other, and occasionally murdered each other in front of the boy on the throne. By the time he was thirteen, Ivan had ordered his first killing himself: Prince Andrei Shuisky, thrown to the dogs. The chronicles say the act surprised no one and stopped no one. The factions kept fighting.

What he learned in those years he never unlearned. The world was a place of plots. Loyalty was a costume people put on in the morning and took off at night. The men who knelt to kiss your hand were measuring your throat.

In January 1547, at sixteen, he was crowned in the Dormition Cathedral with a new title. Not Grand Prince of Moscow, as his father and grandfather had been, but Tsar of all the Russias. The word was a Russified contraction of Caesar, and the choice was deliberate. Constantinople had fallen to the Ottomans almost a century earlier; the eastern Roman Empire was gone; Moscow, by this reckoning, was the third Rome and its ruler the legitimate heir of the Caesars and of the Byzantine emperors. A young man with a wounded childhood was being told, in the most public ceremony his realm could produce, that he was God's chosen sovereign over a chosen people.

A few weeks later he married Anastasia Romanovna, of the Romanov family. She was, by every account, the one person in his life who could calm him. They had six children. Most died young.

The first years of his rule were the good years - the years his later admirers would point to when they wanted to argue that Ivan had not always been a monster. He summoned an assembly of the land, the Zemsky Sobor, the first of its kind. He issued a new legal code in 1550. He reorganized the army, creating the streltsy, a permanent corps of musketeers paid from the treasury. He worked with a small circle of advisers - the priest Sylvester, the courtier Alexei Adashev, the Metropolitan Macarius - who later writers would call the Chosen Council, though the name is theirs, not his.

For a moment, in the early 1550s, it looked as if Russia might be governed by something other than fear. The young Tsar was reading, building, reforming. He was also looking east, where the open steppe began at the edge of his own forests, and where the heirs of the Mongols still held the cities along the Volga.

Conquests at Kazan and Astrakhan

Kazan sat on a bluff above the Volga, about five hundred miles east of Moscow, and for as long as anyone in Moscow could remember it had been a problem. The khanate that ruled it was a successor state of the Golden Horde, its rulers Tatar, its faith Islam, its raiding parties a regular feature of life in the Russian east. Slaves taken from Russian villages were sold in Kazan's markets. Russian princes who lost wars there came home without their crowns and sometimes without their heads.

Ivan tried twice to take the city and failed. The third attempt, in the summer of 1552, was different. He brought a hundred and fifty thousand men, by the contemporary estimates, and a corps of foreign engineers who knew how to dig siege works and lay mines. They built a wooden fortress upstream at Sviyazhsk, floated it down the river in pieces, and reassembled it within sight of the walls. They cut off the water supply. They tunneled under the gates and packed the tunnels with powder.

The assault came in early October. The explosions brought down a section of wall; the streltsy went in through the breach; the fighting in the streets lasted most of the day. By evening the khan was a prisoner and the city was burning. Ivan ordered a cathedral built on Red Square to commemorate the victory. It still stands, the building most foreigners picture when they picture Moscow, its onion domes painted in colors that had not yet been invented when the original was completed.

Astrakhan came four years later and required almost no fighting. The khanate at the mouth of the Volga had been weakened by its own internal quarrels, and when Russian forces appeared in 1556 the city was effectively abandoned to them. With Astrakhan in Russian hands, the entire length of the Volga - from the forests of the north to the Caspian Sea - was open to Russian boats, Russian merchants, and Russian settlers.

The consequences were larger than the campaigns. For the first time, a Russian state ruled substantial Muslim populations, and ruled them as subjects rather than tributaries. The frontier moved. Cossacks pushed south and east along the new rivers. Within a generation, freebooters in Russian pay would be crossing the Urals into Siberia, where the small khanate at Sibir would fall to a few hundred men under the Cossack Yermak. Russia was becoming, almost without noticing it, a Eurasian land empire.

The conquests also changed how Ivan understood himself. He had taken cities that had once taken tribute from his ancestors. He had reversed, on the ground, the humiliation of the Mongol yoke. The chroniclers compared him to David and to Constantine. Western visitors who reached his court in these years - English merchants from the new Muscovy Company, German envoys, Italian craftsmen - found a ruler who received them in robes of cloth-of-gold and expected to be addressed as a brother sovereign of the Holy Roman Emperor.

Then, in 1560, Anastasia died. Ivan was certain she had been poisoned by the boyars. Modern testing of her remains in the twentieth century turned up unusually high levels of mercury, which proves nothing but does not exactly contradict him. Whatever the cause, the man who walked away from her funeral was not the man who had walked into it. Sylvester was exiled to a monastery. Adashev was arrested and died in prison. The Chosen Council, if it had ever really existed as such, was finished.

The Oprichnina: Russia's First Terror

In December 1564, without warning, the Tsar left Moscow. He took his family, his treasury, his icons, and a heavy guard. He went to Alexandrov, a fortified settlement about seventy miles to the northeast, and from there he sent two letters back to the capital. The first, addressed to the boyars and the clergy, accused them of treason, theft, and indifference to the suffering of the realm. The second, addressed to the common people of Moscow, explained that he held no grievance against them but could no longer rule over traitors and was therefore abdicating.

It was theater, and it worked. Delegations rode out to Alexandrov to beg him to return. He agreed, but only on conditions. He would have absolute power to punish whom he chose. And he would carve out, from within the existing realm, a private kingdom of his own.

This was the oprichnina, from a Russian word meaning "the part set aside." Whole districts - the best lands, the wealthiest towns, the lucrative northern trade routes - were taken into the Tsar's personal domain, administered by his own men and answerable only to him. The rest of the country, called the zemshchina, was left to be governed in the old way by the boyar council. Within the oprichnina, the great families were dispossessed; their estates were given to a new class of servitors, men with no inherited rank, who held their lands at the Tsar's pleasure and would lose them the moment they displeased him.

These were the oprichniki. They dressed in black. They rode black horses. To their saddles they tied a dog's head and a broom, the first to sniff out the Tsar's enemies, the second to sweep them away. They numbered perhaps six thousand at the height. They included Russian nobles, foreign adventurers like the German Heinrich von Staden, who later wrote a chilling memoir of his time among them, and at their head the Tsar's favorite enforcer, Malyuta Skuratov, a man whose name still functions in Russian as a shorthand for a torturer.

What followed has no clean equivalent in earlier European history. The oprichniki rode through villages and confiscated, raped, and killed. They executed boyars on charges that were sometimes invented and sometimes not. They tortured priests. They drowned families together in sacks. Ivan watched, and sometimes participated. He had developed a habit, in these years, of alternating between violence and ostentatious religious devotion, retiring to monastic cells to read the lives of the saints, then emerging to order fresh executions.

The worst single episode came in the winter of 1569-1570. Convinced that the city of Novgorod was conspiring to defect to Lithuania - the charge was almost certainly false - Ivan led the oprichniki north. They sealed the city. For five weeks they killed. Estimates of the dead range from a few thousand to over fifteen thousand, and the chroniclers describe bodies being thrown from a bridge into the Volkhov River in such numbers that the current was blocked. The archbishop was paraded through the streets sewn into a bearskin and hunted with dogs. The city never recovered its standing. The northern trading network that had begun with the Hanseatic merchants of the medieval Republic was effectively destroyed by Russian hands.

The oprichnina ended almost as suddenly as it had begun. In 1571 the Crimean Tatars raided Moscow, burning most of the city while the oprichnina army failed to intercept them. The following year, when the Tatars came again, it was a combined force of oprichniki and regular troops, under the command of a zemshchina prince, that defeated them at the Battle of Molodi. The lesson was hard to miss. Ivan disbanded the oprichnina that same year and forbade its name from being spoken. Many of the men who had served him most loyally were quietly killed.

What had been destroyed could not be rebuilt. The old aristocracy was broken as a political force. The pattern of rule by terror - of a sovereign who could reach into any household at any time - had been demonstrated and would not be forgotten. Russian autocracy as a working system, not as an idea but as a thing that ran on fear of the man at the top, was now in place.

The Livonian War and Imperial Ambition

The Baltic in the sixteenth century was where the money was. Furs, wax, timber, grain, and naval stores moved through its ports to the markets of Antwerp and London. Russia had no port of its own on it. To trade with the West, Russian merchants depended on the towns of the Livonian Confederation, a loose collection of bishoprics and Teutonic Order territories along the eastern Baltic coast, and on whatever tariffs and indignities those towns chose to impose.

In 1558 Ivan invaded. The pretext was an unpaid tribute; the goal was the coast. The first years went well. Russian armies took Narva, took Dorpat, pushed deep into Livonia, and for a brief moment it appeared that the Tsar might end the war with his own harbors on the Baltic and his own ships unloading at his own quays. Then the war became something else. The collapse of the Livonian Order was so complete that it sucked in every neighboring power. Sweden took the north. Denmark took islands. Poland and Lithuania, joined formally in 1569 as the Polish-Lithuanian Commonwealth, took the south. What had begun as a campaign against a weak adversary became a war against a coalition of stronger ones.

It dragged on for twenty-five years. The Russian treasury emptied. The peasantry, taxed beyond what the land could bear and conscripted into armies that never came home, began to drift south, away from the heartland, toward the steppe frontier where the Cossacks lived. Famine and plague did the rest. By the late 1570s, whole districts of the northern Russian countryside were depopulated.

The decisive turn came when Stephen Báthory, an able Transylvanian elected King of Poland in 1576, took personal command of the Commonwealth's armies. Báthory was the kind of opponent Ivan had not faced before: disciplined, professional, comfortable with siege warfare in the Western style. He recaptured Polotsk in 1579. He took Velikiye Luki in 1580. In 1581 he laid siege to Pskov, one of the great fortified cities of the Russian north, and although the garrison held out through a brutal winter, Ivan understood that he had lost.

The Truce of Yam-Zapolsky in 1582 surrendered all the Livonian conquests to Poland. The armistice with Sweden the following year gave up the Russian towns on the Gulf of Finland. After a quarter-century of war, Russia's coastline on the Baltic was smaller than it had been when Ivan began. The empire that had swallowed Kazan and Astrakhan was unable to hold a single harbor on the western sea.

The failure mattered for reasons that went beyond geography. Ivan had staked his claim to imperial standing on the ability to deal with European sovereigns as an equal. He had corresponded with Elizabeth of England, scolded the Swedish king for his low birth, lectured the Polish nobility on the proper relationship between monarchs and subjects. The Livonian War was supposed to be the proof. It became the disproof. The next Tsar who tried to reach the Baltic would do so a century later, and his name would be Peter.

Death of a Dynasty

In November 1581, in his private apartments, Ivan struck his eldest son with an iron-tipped staff. The blow caught the young man on the temple. He lingered for several days and then died.

The accounts of what provoked the quarrel vary. One version says the Tsar had struck his pregnant daughter-in-law for dressing immodestly, causing her to miscarry, and that his son had confronted him over it. Another says the argument was political, over the conduct of the war. The Tsarevich Ivan Ivanovich was twenty-seven, intelligent, by some accounts the only person his father still listened to. He was also the only competent heir.

What was left was Fyodor, the second son, gentle, slow, more interested in bell-ringing than in government, and Dmitry, an infant born to Ivan's seventh wife in a marriage the Church had never recognized. The dynasty that had ruled Moscow since the days of Daniel, son of Alexander Nevsky - the line called the Rurikids, traced back by legend to the Varangian prince who had come to Novgorod in the ninth century - was running out of competent men in a single afternoon's rage.

Ivan never recovered from the killing. Contemporaries describe him in the last years as physically broken, his hair and beard gone white, his body swollen and stinking from some disease modern observers have variously diagnosed as syphilis, mercury poisoning from his own medicines, or simply the accumulated wreckage of his life. He had outlived seven wives. He had killed his own son. He had emptied his treasury fighting a war he lost. The court around him was a court of survivors, men who had learned to be useful by being silent.

He died in March 1584, while setting up a chessboard. He was fifty-three.

Fyodor was crowned in his place. He prayed, he rang bells, he left the governing to his brother-in-law, a former oprichnik named Boris Godunov, who managed the realm with intelligence and care for the next fourteen years. In 1591, in the town of Uglich, the half-brother Dmitry was found in a courtyard with his throat cut. The official inquiry, headed by men loyal to Godunov, ruled it an accident: an epileptic seizure during a game with a knife. Few believed it then. Fewer believe it now. The truth was buried with the boy.

Fyodor died childless in 1598. The Rurikid line, which had ruled in Moscow for more than seven centuries by the longest reckoning, ended in a quiet bedchamber with no clear successor. Boris Godunov was elected Tsar by an assembly summoned for the purpose. He was an able man, but he was not of the old blood, and within a few years of his own death the country would discover what it meant to have an autocracy without a legitimate autocrat.

In a monastery north of Moscow, a monk who had once been a minor nobleman began to take an interest in the question of what had really happened at Uglich. He would, in time, claim to be Dmitry himself, miraculously saved. He would not be the last to make the claim. The forge had done its work. What came out of it now had to be lived with.

The forge had done its work, and what came out of it had to be lived with. An autocracy had been built that needed an autocrat, and the line of men entitled to fill that role had narrowed almost to a point. When the point disappeared, when the last Rurikid closed his eyes in 1598 without a son, the machinery did not stop. It kept turning, demanding a tsar, and the country began to discover what it cost to feed that machinery with men who had no claim to the throne but their own ambition and the willingness of others to believe them.

Chapter 5
The Time of Troubles

Boris Godunov and the Coming Crisis

In January 1598, Tsar Feodor I died without leaving a son. He had been a frail, pious man, more comfortable ringing church bells than governing, and for years the actual business of ruling had fallen to his brother-in-law, a clever boyar named Boris Godunov. Now the line of Rurik, which had given Russia its princes for seven centuries, ended in an empty cradle.

The Assembly of the Land elected Godunov tsar. He had the experience, the network, and the temperament for the job. What he did not have was the one thing that mattered most in Muscovy: blood. He was not descended from Rurik. Every boyar family with a longer pedigree - and there were many - regarded him as a usurper dressed in borrowed robes.

For the first two years, Godunov ruled competently. He pursued cautious diplomacy with Sweden and Poland, encouraged foreign craftsmen to settle in Moscow, and sent young Russians abroad to study, a startling experiment that ended badly when most of them refused to come home. He built fortresses on the southern frontier and pushed Russian settlement deeper into Siberia. None of it would matter, because in the summer of 1601 it began to rain and did not stop.

The rains lasted ten weeks. What survived rotted in the fields. Then, in the middle of August, the frost came, weeks early, and killed everything that had begun to ripen. The next year was no better, and the year after that worse still. Contemporary chroniclers describe people boiling tree bark, eating hay, eating each other. In Moscow, Godunov opened the granaries and distributed silver to the poor, which only drew more starving peasants into the city, where they died in the streets faster than the carts could carry them out. The official count of bodies buried at state expense in Moscow alone reached over a hundred thousand. Across the realm, perhaps two million people died, roughly a third of the population.

A famine on that scale is not only a catastrophe of food. It is a catastrophe of belief. In a world where the tsar was God's anointed and the harvest was God's gift, a famine that lasted three years could mean only one thing: the man on the throne was not the rightful one. The rumors had always been there. Now they hardened into conviction.

Those rumors concerned a boy. In 1591, Feodor's half-brother Dmitry, the youngest son of Ivan the Terrible, had died in the town of Uglich at the age of nine. The official inquiry, conducted by a commission that Godunov himself dispatched, concluded that the child had stabbed himself in the throat during an epileptic fit while playing with a knife. Few people believed it then. Fewer believed it now. The story that circulated in the markets and monasteries was simpler: Boris had ordered the boy killed to clear his own path to the throne.

Whether Godunov was guilty has never been settled. Historians differ on whether he ordered the killing, knew of it, or had nothing to do with it at all. What is certain is that by 1603, with corpses in the snow and brigands forming armies in the forests, a great many Russians had decided that he was guilty, and that God was punishing the land for tolerating him.

It was in that climate, in the spring of 1603, in a monastery on the Polish-Lithuanian border, that a young man let slip a startling claim. He had not died at Uglich, he said. He had been smuggled away. He was Dmitry, the true tsarevich, and he had come back for what was his.

The False Dmitrys

The young man's name, by most accounts, was Grigory Otrepyev, a defrocked monk from a minor noble family. He had served briefly in the household of the Romanovs before fleeing east, and he knew enough about court life to play the part. The Polish magnates who received him were not fools. They probably did not believe him either. But they understood the value of a plausible pretender, and they had been looking for a reason to interfere in Russian affairs for a long time.

One of them, the voivode Jerzy Mniszech, agreed to back the pretender in exchange for two things: the hand of his daughter Marina, who would become tsarina, and a generous territorial settlement once Dmitry sat on the throne. The pretender, for his part, secretly converted to Catholicism and promised the papal nuncio that he would bring Russia into communion with Rome. In October 1604, with about four thousand Polish volunteers, Cossacks, and Russian exiles, he crossed the border.

By any reasonable military calculation he should have been crushed within weeks. Godunov sent armies many times the size of his against him. They lost. Towns opened their gates. Garrisons defected. Peasants who had eaten bark the winter before saw in this stranger the answer to their prayers. The closer he came to Moscow, the larger his army grew.

In April 1605, Boris Godunov died suddenly at dinner, possibly of a stroke, possibly poisoned. His sixteen-year-old son Feodor II was proclaimed tsar and lasted seven weeks. The boyars in Moscow read the wind, abandoned the boy, and arranged for him and his mother to be strangled in their chambers. On July 18, the pretender entered Moscow at the head of his army. The widow of Ivan the Terrible, brought out of her convent, embraced him publicly as her son. Whether she did so under duress, or because grief had made her willing, no one knows.

He was crowned tsar. For about ten months he ruled, and by the standards of what came before and after, he ruled well. He pardoned exiles, including the Romanovs. He doubled the salaries of state officials. He held open audiences where ordinary petitioners could speak to him directly. He was, by all accounts, intelligent and energetic. He was also, fatally, foreign in his habits. He did not nap after dinner. He did not bathe in the Russian way. He brought Polish guards into the Kremlin. And in May 1606 he married Marina Mniszech in a Catholic ceremony in the Russian capital, an act that scandalized the Orthodox clergy and the Moscow crowds in roughly equal measure.

Eight days after the wedding, before dawn, the boyar Vasily Shuisky led a conspiracy into the Kremlin. The pretender tried to escape through a window, broke his leg in the fall, and was shot in the courtyard. His body was dragged through the streets, burned, the ashes mixed with gunpowder and fired from a cannon back in the direction of Poland.

Shuisky took the throne. He was not the answer either. Within a year a second pretender appeared, also calling himself Dmitry, claiming to have escaped the Kremlin yet again. Marina Mniszech, brought out of detention, recognized him as her husband. So did much of southern Russia. He set up court at the village of Tushino, a few miles from Moscow, where he held parallel sway over half the country for nearly two years and became known to history as the Tushino Brigand. A third Dmitry appeared later in Pskov and was briefly accepted there. Cossack bands roamed the steppe in his various names. Towns swore allegiance to one pretender on Monday and another on Friday. The country was no longer governed in any meaningful sense. It was contested.

Polish Occupation of the Kremlin

In 1609, with the Tushino camp swelling and his own authority collapsing, Tsar Vasily Shuisky did the one thing guaranteed to make matters worse. He signed a treaty with Sweden, offering territory in exchange for soldiers. King Sigismund III of Poland, who was at war with Sweden and had been waiting for an opening, now had his pretext. He crossed the border with a real army, not a handful of volunteers, and laid siege to Smolensk.

The Tushino camp dissolved. The second false Dmitry fled south, where he was murdered the following year by one of his own Tatar guards. Some of his Russian supporters, despairing of finding a tsar at home, made an extraordinary offer to Sigismund: they would accept the Polish king's son, the fifteen-year-old Wladyslaw, as tsar of Russia, provided he converted to Orthodoxy and respected Russian custom. In February 1610, a treaty to that effect was signed outside Smolensk.

In Moscow, the boyars decided this was the least bad option available. They deposed Shuisky in July, shaved his head, and shut him in a monastery. He would die in Polish captivity. The boyar council - the so-called Seven Boyars - then opened the gates of the Kremlin to a Polish garrison commanded by Stanislaw Zolkiewski, on the understanding that Wladyslaw would arrive shortly and rule as a proper Orthodox tsar.

Wladyslaw did not arrive. Sigismund had changed his mind. He wanted the Russian throne for himself, and he had no intention of letting his son convert to a heretical church. The Polish garrison stayed. The promised tsar did not come. Russia now had foreign Catholic troops occupying the Kremlin, a Polish king claiming the throne from outside the country, and no Russian sovereign of any kind.

What happened next was the thing nobody in the boyar council had calculated for. The Patriarch of Moscow, Hermogen, an old man of about eighty, refused to recognize Sigismund's claim. From his cell in the Kremlin, where the Poles soon placed him under arrest, he began sending letters out into the country. He addressed them to the towns of the north and east, to the merchants and the lesser gentry and the parish priests. He told them that the faith was in danger, that the foreigners in Moscow were heretics, that Russia must rise. The letters were copied and recopied in monastery scriptoriums and carried by riders along the frozen rivers. Hermogen would die of starvation in his cell in February 1612. By then his letters had done their work.

Minin, Pozharsky, and the Liberation of Moscow

A first militia, raised in 1611 from the Ryazan lands, marched on Moscow and reached the city. It fell apart in front of the Kremlin walls in quarrels between its noble and Cossack factions, and its leader was murdered by his own men. The Poles still held the Kremlin. The capital was a ruin of burned wards and roving bands.

The second militia began in Nizhny Novgorod, a trading town on the Volga, in the autumn of 1611. A butcher named Kuzma Minin, recently elected to a minor town office, stood up in the marketplace and proposed that the citizens tax themselves, by a third of their property, to raise an army. He proposed it more than once, and kept proposing it until they agreed. Tradition holds that when some refused, Minin offered up his own savings first, then his house, then his wife's jewelry, and shamed the rest into following. The town records do not confirm every detail, but they confirm the substance: Nizhny Novgorod taxed itself to raise a force.

For a commander they sought out Prince Dmitry Pozharsky, a minor Rurikid noble who had been wounded leading street fighting against the Poles in Moscow the previous year and was recovering on his estate. He was not a famous general. He was known to be honest, which was rarer and, in 1611, more valuable. He accepted on the condition that Minin handle the finances, which Minin did with a clerk's precision.

Through the winter and spring of 1612, the militia moved north along the Volga, gathering men and money in Yaroslavl, where it set up a provisional government and minted its own coins. By August it was outside Moscow. A Polish relief army under Hetman Chodkiewicz arrived at the same time, carrying provisions for the starving garrison in the Kremlin. The battles that followed, fought in the streets and fields around the city walls over several days, were among the most savage of the entire decade. Pozharsky's men, reinforced at the critical moment by Cossacks who had wavered and then chose their side, beat the relief army back. Chodkiewicz withdrew with his wagons intact but his mission failed.

Inside the Kremlin, the garrison began to starve. The accounts that survive describe the eating of leather, of rats, and at the end, of one another. On November 4, 1612, by the Julian calendar Russia still used, the gates opened and the survivors came out. Pozharsky entered the Kremlin. The Polish soldiers were spared, against the wishes of much of his own army, and most were eventually sent home.

The Kremlin churches had been stripped. The royal treasury was empty. In the Cathedral of the Dormition, where the tsars had been crowned for two centuries, the icons had been pried from their settings and the silver melted down. A service of thanksgiving was held in the wreckage. The date is still observed in Russia as a national holiday.

The Romanovs Take the Throne

Liberating Moscow was not the same as governing Russia. The country had no tsar, no functioning treasury, no clear principle by which to choose a sovereign. In January 1613, an Assembly of the Land was summoned to Moscow. It was larger and broader than any such assembly before it, drawing delegates from the towns, the gentry, the clergy, the Cossacks, and even the state peasantry. Some seven hundred men crowded into the city, lodging where they could in the half-burned houses, and began to argue.

They argued for weeks. Several candidates were proposed. A Swedish prince was suggested and rejected; the country had had enough of foreign princes. Prince Pozharsky's name was put forward and, by most accounts, he declined it. Various boyar families pressed their own claims and canceled each other out.

The name that emerged was Michael Romanov. He was sixteen years old. He was the great-nephew of Ivan the Terrible's first and beloved wife, Anastasia Romanovna, which gave him the thinnest possible thread of connection to the old dynasty. His father, Feodor Romanov, had been forced into monastic vows by Boris Godunov years before, taken the name Filaret, and was now a prisoner in Poland. The boy himself was at the Ipatiev Monastery near Kostroma, with his mother, when the delegation arrived to inform him that he had been chosen.

Both he and his mother are said to have wept and refused. The delegation insisted. The mother warned that the boy was too young, that the boyars were treacherous, that the country was ruined. She was right on all three counts. In the end she relented and gave her blessing before the icon of the Mother of God of Saint Theodore, which would remain a Romanov family treasure for the next three hundred years.

Michael was crowned in the Cathedral of the Dormition on July 22, 1613. The cathedral had been hastily repaired. The crown itself had been cobbled together from what could be found, because the original regalia were gone. The boy who wore it could barely read state documents and signed almost nothing on his own authority for the first years of his reign. The country he inherited was depopulated, indebted, partly occupied by Swedes in the north and Poles in the west. The wars with both would drag on for years. His father Filaret, when he was eventually returned in a prisoner exchange in 1619, would take effective control of the government and rule in his son's name as Patriarch.

At the Ipatiev Monastery, after the delegation left, a young woman who had been in service to the Romanov household swept up the cathedral floor where the boy had knelt. The candles were taken down and counted. The icons were put back in their cases. Outside, the snow that had been falling all afternoon was beginning to settle on the rooftops, and on the long road south toward Moscow.

The candles were counted and put back in their cases, the icons returned to their stands, and a boy who had not asked to be tsar rode south through the snow toward Moscow. The dynasty that began in the Ipatiev cathedral that winter would last three hundred years. Its first decades were spent in recovery: armies rebuilt, borders patched, a father ruling in his son's name. Recovery, though, was not the same as ambition. The Romanov who would force his country to look outward, who would build ships and cut beards and drag his nobles into a wider world, was still two generations away.

Chapter 6
Peter the Great and the Window to the West

The Grand Embassy

In the spring of 1697, a tall young man calling himself Peter Mikhailov boarded a coach in Moscow and set off for the West. The alias fooled no one. He stood six and a half feet, towered over every retinue he met, and travelled with a suite of two hundred and fifty Russians whose purpose was openly diplomatic. But the fiction mattered to him. As Peter Mikhailov he could walk into a shipyard, take an axe in his hands, and learn a trade. As tsar he could only be received, fed, and toasted.

He was twenty-four. His mother had died three years earlier, leaving him at last in sole possession of the throne he had nominally shared since the age of nine with his sickly half-brother Ivan V and, in practice, with the regent Sofia. He had spent his youth in the German Quarter outside Moscow, drinking with Dutch shipwrights and Scottish soldiers, sailing a small English boat on a lake near Pereslavl, and drilling his play-regiments until they became something more dangerous than play. He had grown up wanting to know how things worked: locks, gunpowder, dentistry, ship timbers, lathes. Now he wanted to know how Europe worked.

The Grand Embassy had an official purpose, which was to build a coalition against the Ottoman Empire. It failed in that purpose almost immediately. The European powers were preoccupied with the coming question of the Spanish succession and had no appetite for a southern war on behalf of Moscow. But Peter had given himself a second mission, and that one succeeded beyond anything Russia had attempted before.

He went to the shipyards of the Dutch East India Company in Amsterdam and worked for four months as a carpenter. He took notes on the design of hulls, the cut of sails, the discipline of the yards. When he decided the Dutch built by intuition rather than mathematics, he moved on to England, where the Royal Navy taught its shipwrights to draft plans on paper. In Deptford he lived in the house of the diarist John Evelyn, whose gardener afterwards complained that the Russians had turned the lawn into mud and the hedges into firewood. Peter went to the Royal Mint, to the Royal Society, to the observatory at Greenwich, to a foundry, to an anatomy theatre where he is said to have helped with a dissection.

He recruited as he went. Engineers, navigators, gunners, doctors, mathematicians, architects - hundreds of foreign specialists were hired into Russian service. He bought instruments, weapons, books. He brought back the trades themselves, the men who could practise them, and the assumption that knowledge was something a sovereign acquired by going to it rather than waiting for it to arrive.

In the summer of 1698 a courier reached him in Vienna with news that the streltsy, the old musketeer regiments in Moscow, had mutinied. He turned for home immediately, abandoning a planned trip to Venice. By the time he reached Moscow the revolt had already been crushed, but Peter ordered a fresh round of investigations, torture, and executions. More than a thousand streltsy were put to death; their bodies hung for months outside the walls of the Kremlin and beneath Sofia's convent window. The regiments were dissolved.

Then he summoned his nobles and cut off their beards.

The story is famous because it actually happened, in the long room of the palace at Preobrazhenskoe, with Peter wielding the shears himself. A beard tax followed for those who wished to keep them. Long Russian kaftans were shortened by decree. The calendar was changed so that the year began in January rather than September. None of this was cosmetic. Peter had come back from the West convinced that the surface of a country and its substance were not separable, and that if he could not change what his nobles thought, he would begin by changing how they looked.

War with Sweden and the Battle of Poltava

The war that defined his reign began the following year, and it began badly.

In 1700, Peter joined Denmark and Saxony in a coalition against Sweden, expecting an easy partition of the Baltic provinces of a young and untested king. Charles XII was eighteen. He turned out to be one of the most brilliant battlefield commanders of his age. Within months he had knocked Denmark out of the war. In November he marched on the Russian army besieging the fortress of Narva on the Gulf of Finland, fell upon it through a snowstorm, and routed a force four times the size of his own. Russian artillery, Russian officers, Russian command - all of it disintegrated. Peter himself had left the camp the day before, a decision that his enemies called cowardice and his admirers called prudence. The whole campaign was a humiliation.

Charles, satisfied that the Russians were finished, turned south to deal with Augustus of Saxony. He would spend the next six years chasing Augustus across Poland, and those six years were the gift that saved Peter.

He used them. The army was rebuilt almost from scratch. Conscription was systematised: one recruit from every twenty peasant households, taken for life. Foreign officers drilled the new regiments in line tactics. Church bells were melted down to cast cannon. Iron foundries went up in the Urals under the direction of the Demidov family, who would grow rich on the contracts. By 1704 Russian forces had taken Narva back. By 1708 they had stopped a Swedish supply train at the Battle of Lesnaya, depriving Charles's main army of food and powder as it pushed eastward into Ukraine.

Charles had decided to march on Moscow. The Ukrainian hetman Mazepa had promised to bring the Cossacks over to his side, and a southern route through fertile country seemed safer than a winter advance through the burned Russian borderlands. Mazepa, as it turned out, could deliver only a fraction of what he had promised. The winter of 1708-1709 was the coldest in living memory across Europe; birds fell frozen out of the air in Paris. The Swedish army that emerged in the spring was weakened, hungry, and far from home.

In June 1709 it laid siege to the small fortress of Poltava on the Vorskla River. Peter brought up the main Russian army - some forty thousand men, with over a hundred guns - and dug in across the open ground north of the town. Charles, wounded in the foot a few days earlier, was carried into the battle on a litter. His infantry numbered fewer than twenty thousand. He attacked anyway.

The Swedes broke through the first line of Russian redoubts at dawn on 27 June. Then the killing ground opened in front of them. Russian artillery, ranged and prepared, tore the Swedish columns apart before they could close. The infantry that followed up was disciplined, well-supplied, and three times more numerous than what was left of Charles's army. By midday it was over. Several thousand Swedes lay dead on the field; most of the survivors surrendered three days later at Perevolochna on the Dnieper. Charles escaped south into Ottoman territory with a small escort and would not see Sweden again for five years.

Poltava ended Swedish dominance in northern Europe. It did not end the war, which dragged on for another twelve years through a Turkish campaign that Peter nearly lost on the Prut River, through naval battles in the Baltic - Gangut in 1714 was the first great Russian victory at sea - and through the slow grinding-down of Swedish positions in Finland and along the coast. The Treaty of Nystad in 1721 confirmed what Poltava had decided. Russia took Livonia, Estonia, Ingria, and a strip of Karelia. The Senate offered Peter the title of Emperor and Father of the Fatherland. He accepted both. He had been at war for twenty-one of the twenty-nine years he had ruled in his own name.

Building St. Petersburg

The new capital was begun before the war was won, in territory that on the maps of 1703 still belonged to Sweden.

Peter laid the first stone of the Peter and Paul Fortress on a small island in the marshes where the Neva River breaks into its delta. The site was almost uninhabitable. It flooded twice a year. The ground was peat and silt for many feet down. There was no stone within easy reach, no firm road, no farmland, and in winter the wind came across the Gulf of Finland with nothing to stop it. The Swedes had held this coast for a century and built almost nothing on it. Peter intended to build a city of two hundred thousand people.

He sent for Italian and French architects. Domenico Trezzini, a Swiss working out of Copenhagen, became the chief builder of the early city and designed the cathedral inside the fortress with its needle-thin gilded spire. Jean-Baptiste Le Blond, a pupil of Le Nôtre, drew the first master plan. The streets were to be straight, the canals geometric, the facades aligned. Wooden building was forbidden in the centre. Every stone-carrying cart entering the city had to deliver a quota of rocks as a toll. Stonemasons throughout the empire were ordered to come north or to send their apprentices.

The labour was conscripted. Peasants were drafted in waves of twenty or thirty thousand at a time, marched up from the interior provinces, and set to draining marshes and driving pilings. They worked in water to their knees through the short summer and slept in earth shelters on the islands. The mortality figures have never been agreed; estimates range from tens of thousands to far more across the early decades. Disease, exhaustion, and the cold did most of the killing. The phrase that attached itself to the place - the city built on bones - was literal as well as figurative. When foundations were dug in the eighteenth century, workers turned up skeletons.

Peter loved it. He built himself a small log cabin near the river in the first months of construction and lived in it while he supervised.

He chose the location of bridges, the angle of streets, the design of his own modest summer palace. He took particular pleasure in the shipyards on the Admiralty side, where the navy he had been imagining since boyhood was actually taking shape. By 1712 the court had been moved north from Moscow. The boyar families, who detested the new place, were ordered to build stone houses there according to standard plans depending on their rank. Foreign merchants were encouraged to settle. Embassies followed.

The result was unlike anything else in Russia. Moscow had grown in concentric rings around the Kremlin over five centuries, with twisting lanes and onion domes and wooden quarters that burned every generation. St. Petersburg was drawn on paper before it was built. Its skyline was horizontal where Moscow's was vertical, its colours pale yellow and pale green where Moscow's were red and gold, its churches Italian-Baroque where Moscow's were Byzantine. Foreigners arriving by sea said it looked European. Russians arriving by road said it looked like something that should not exist.

It was the window Peter had wanted, opened by force in a place where no city ought to have stood. The fact that it stood at all was the point. He had decided that Russia would face the sea and the West, and he had built a capital that could not face anywhere else. By the time he died in 1725, more than forty thousand people lived there. Within a century it would be the fourth largest city in Europe.

Reforming State and Church

The capital was a building. The state Peter was constructing inside it was something harder to see.

The old administration was a tangle of overlapping prikazy, chancelleries that had grown up over generations to handle whatever business arose, each with its own staff and its own jealous traditions. Peter dismantled them. In their place he created colleges - boards on the Swedish model, each responsible for a single domain: war, navy, foreign affairs, commerce, mines, justice. Each was headed by a president and run by a committee, with written procedures and chains of accountability. Above them sat the Senate, which Peter established in 1711 as a standing body to govern in his absence on campaign and which became, in effect, the permanent executive of the empire.

He divided the country into provinces, then redivided them when the first scheme proved unworkable. He imposed a new tax in 1718, the soul tax, levied on every male peasant rather than on households, which roughly doubled state revenue and required a census of the entire serf population. The census itself was a piece of state-building: to count souls one had to define them, and after 1718 the legal categories of serf, state peasant, townsman, and noble became sharper and harder to escape.

The most consequential reform was the Table of Ranks, promulgated in 1722. It set out fourteen parallel grades in the military, civil, and court services, and it laid down that a man's standing depended on the rank he had reached, not the family he had been born into. A commoner who reached the eighth grade in the civil service became a hereditary noble. Existing nobles who never entered service forfeited their precedence. In a single document Peter had subordinated the boyar order to the needs of the state and made nobility itself a function of work.

The work was compulsory. Nobles owed lifelong service from adolescence onward, in the army, the navy, or the bureaucracy. Their sons were registered at birth and inspected periodically; failure to appear at the muster cost an estate. Sons of provincial gentry were ordered abroad to study navigation, mathematics, and engineering, and forbidden to marry until they had passed their examinations. Some learned a great deal. Many learned to mimic the forms of learning. Either way the principle was fixed: the nobility existed because the state required it to exist.

The Church proved harder, but Peter was patient with it. The Patriarch Adrian died in 1700, and Peter simply did not appoint a successor. For two decades the patriarchal throne sat empty while a deputy administered routine business. In 1721 Peter abolished the office altogether. In its place he established the Holy Synod, a board of bishops and lay officials run on the same collegial principles as the rest of the government, with a layman called the Ober-Procurator sitting at its head as the tsar's eyes. The autocephalous Russian Orthodox Church, which had once been a partner of the throne, became a department of the empire.

The theologian Feofan Prokopovich, a Ukrainian whom Peter had brought north and made the chief intellectual defender of his reforms, wrote the document - the Spiritual Regulation - that justified the change. It argued that monarchy by a single God-given ruler was theologically superior to government by a single God-given prelate. The argument was convenient. It was also, in the form Prokopovich gave it, an unmistakably modern piece of political theory, drawing on Hobbes and Pufendorf as much as on the Church Fathers. Peter had not separated church and state. He had absorbed one into the other.

The Cost of Modernization

What it cost the people who lived through it is the hardest part of the story to tell, because most of them left no record.

The soul tax alone took roughly three-quarters of a serf household's surplus in a normal year. War recruitment took the strongest sons for life - in practice, since few survived twenty-five years of campaigning. Forced labour drafts pulled peasants away to St. Petersburg, to the Urals foundries, to the canal works at Lake Ladoga and the Volga-Don portage. Many never returned. Those who did sometimes came back to find their farms abandoned and their families dispersed.

Resistance ran underneath everything. The Old Believers, the schismatic Orthodox who had broken with the church reforms of the previous generation, multiplied in the forests and along the Volga, and some of them concluded that Peter was the Antichrist. The beard tax, the new calendar, the foreign clothes, the Latin alphabet creeping into official documents - all of it was evidence enough. Some Old Believer communities burned themselves alive rather than submit to the new census. The Bashkirs revolted between 1704 and 1711. The Don Cossacks rose under Kondraty Bulavin in 1707-1708, in the middle of the Swedish war, and had to be put down by an army Peter could barely spare. In Astrakhan the streltsy rebelled again. Each revolt was crushed. Each crushing was thorough.

The cruellest episode was inside the tsar's own family. His eldest son Alexei, the child of his first marriage, had grown up devout, traditionalist, and afraid of his father. In 1716 Alexei fled abroad, sheltering first in Vienna and then in Naples. Peter's agents tracked him down and persuaded him to return on a promise of pardon. The promise was not kept. Alexei was interrogated, tortured to extract the names of supposed accomplices, and condemned to death by a tribunal of senators and bishops. He died in the Peter and Paul Fortress in June 1718, before the sentence could be carried out, and the official cause was given as a stroke. Almost no one believed it.

Peter never named a successor. In 1722 he issued a decree giving the reigning monarch the right to choose any heir; he simply never used it. When he died in February 1725, after catching cold wading into the icy Neva to help rescue a foundering boat full of soldiers, the question of the throne was left to the guards regiments and the courtiers around his bed. They chose his widow, a Lithuanian peasant woman he had married for love, who became Catherine I.

He was fifty-two. He had ruled in his own name for thirty-one years. He had nearly tripled state revenue, multiplied the army several times over, created a navy where there had been none, taken the Baltic coast, founded a city, rewritten the rules of nobility and church, and exhausted his country.

The bronze statue Catherine the Great would put up to him half a century later shows him on horseback, hand outstretched over the Neva, the horse rearing on the edge of a great granite cliff. The serpent under its hooves is small and almost hidden. The horse has not yet come down.

The bronze horse on the Neva had not yet come down. Peter had left his country a navy, a capital, a nobility in foreign clothes, and an exhaustion that would take a generation to work through. The throne he had reshaped passed through a series of widows, infants, and palace coups, none of which produced a ruler equal to the office he had designed. What it eventually produced was someone he could not have predicted: a minor German princess who had arrived in Russia at fourteen, learned the language, and waited.

Chapter 7
Catherine the Great and the Enlightened Empire

Coup at the Summer Palace

On the morning of 28 June 1762, Catherine left Peterhof in a carriage and rode toward Saint Petersburg dressed in the green uniform of the Preobrazhensky Guards. She was thirty-three. She had been in Russia for eighteen years, married for seventeen, and empress consort for six months. By nightfall she would be empress in her own right, and her husband would be under arrest.

The husband was Peter III, grandson of Peter the Great, nephew of the Empress Elizabeth, and, by Catherine's own later account and that of nearly everyone who met him, a man entirely unsuited to ruling Russia. He admired Frederick the Great of Prussia to the point of worship. When Elizabeth died in January 1762, Russia had been winning its war against Prussia; within months of his accession, Peter had returned the conquered territory and signed an alliance with Berlin. He spoke German by preference, attended Lutheran services, and was said to have mocked the Orthodox clergy to their faces. The Guards regiments, which he proposed to dress in Prussian uniforms and send to fight Denmark over his Holstein inheritance, were ready to be persuaded that another candidate might suit them better.

Catherine had been preparing the persuasion for months. Her lover, Grigory Orlov, was an officer of the Izmailovsky Guards; his brothers Alexei and Fyodor were in other regiments. There were sympathetic ministers, a sympathetic archbishop, and several thousand soldiers ready to swear an oath. When a junior conspirator was arrested on 27 June, the plot had to move at once. Alexei Orlov arrived at Peterhof in the small hours and woke

Catherine with the news. She dressed, climbed into the carriage, and went.

In the capital the regiments took the oath in sequence: Izmailovsky first, then Semyonovsky, then Preobrazhensky. The senate followed. By the time Peter, hunting and drinking at Oranienbaum, understood what was happening, the city had already declared for his wife. He wrote her a letter offering to abdicate if she would let him return to Holstein with his mistress and his violin. She accepted the abdication and ignored the rest. He was taken to a country house at Ropsha under guard.

Eight days later he was dead. The official cause was hemorrhoidal colic, a phrase that fooled no one. Alexei Orlov sent Catherine a half-coherent note describing a drunken quarrel and a struggle in which Peter had somehow ended up strangled. Catherine kept the note. Whether she had ordered the killing, whether she had wanted it but not ordered it, or whether the Orlovs had simply understood what she could not say aloud, is a question historians have never settled. What is certain is that she profited by it, that she punished no one, and that for the rest of her life she lived under the suspicion that her crown had been bought with her husband's blood.

She was crowned in Moscow that September. The ceremony was elaborate and entirely Russian: she walked under a canopy through the Cathedral of the Dormition, took the crown from the metropolitan and placed it on her own head, and emerged into a city that had been told, again and again, that the small German princess who had come to marry Peter was now the legitimate sovereign of Orthodox Russia. Most of those watching had no reason to believe it. She would spend the next thirty-four years making them believe it anyway.

The Empress and the Philosophers

Catherine wrote letters. She wrote them in the morning before her court woke and at night after it slept, in French, on small sheets of paper, in a hand that grew more confident as the years passed. Some of the letters went to her ministers. Many went to Paris.

Voltaire she never met. Their correspondence lasted fifteen years and filled volumes. He called her the Semiramis of the North, compared her to Marcus Aurelius, and accepted her gifts. She sent him furs and praise and detailed accounts of her reforms, and he in turn told the salons of Paris that an enlightened monarch was at last ruling somewhere on earth, even if that somewhere was Russia. When he died in 1778 she bought his library and had it shipped to Saint Petersburg, where it still sits. Diderot she did meet. He came to Russia in 1773, stayed five months, and held long conversations with the empress in her private apartments, during which he was said to grow so excited that he tapped her knees to make his points. She listened - and later observed, in a remark recorded afterward, that the philosopher worked on paper, which suffered everything, while she worked on human skin, which was rather more sensitive.

The remark caught something true about her relationship with the Enlightenment. She read it carefully and quoted it accurately. In 1767 she summoned a Legislative Commission of more than five hundred delegates from across the empire - nobles, townsmen, state peasants, even a handful of non-Russian tribal representatives - and gave them a document she had spent two years writing. It was called the Nakaz, or Instruction, and it borrowed openly from Montesquieu and from the Italian jurist Cesare Beccaria. It denounced torture. It questioned capital punishment. It described a monarchy bound by law and a society in which all subjects, in principle, possessed certain rights. It was so liberal in its language that the French government banned it.

The commission met for a year and a half, produced enormous quantities of testimony about the actual condition of the empire, and was then dissolved without legislating anything. The war with

Turkey was the official reason. The deeper reason was that the delegates, asked what they wanted, had mostly wanted things Catherine could not give. The nobles wanted firmer control over their serfs. The townsmen wanted protection from the nobles. The state peasants wanted relief from taxes. Nobody wanted the abstract liberal monarchy the Nakaz described. The document was filed away and praised abroad.

What Catherine did do, in the years that followed, was build institutions. She founded the Smolny Institute, the first state school for girls in Europe. She reformed the medical service and was inoculated against smallpox in 1768 as a public demonstration, when the procedure was still considered dangerous. She established a network of public schools in provincial towns, expanded the Academy of Sciences, supported the first Russian-language journals, and collected art on a scale that astonished European dealers. The Hermitage began as her private gallery; by the end of her reign it held some of the finest pictures in Europe, bought in bulk from the heirs of Walpole and the bankrupt estates of French aristocrats. She wrote plays, satirical essays, and a history of Russia for her grandchildren, and conducted herself, in the eyes of Europe, as the model of the enlightened sovereign. All of this while the institution of serfdom, on which her entire system rested, grew steadily more oppressive beneath her.

Pugachev's Rebellion

In September 1773 a Don Cossack named Yemelyan Pugachev appeared in the Yaik river country, on the empire's south-eastern edge, and announced that he was Peter III. He had survived, he said. The reports of his death had been lies. He had been wandering in disguise, and now he had come back to reclaim his throne and to free his people from the German woman who had usurped it.

The claim was preposterous on its face. Pugachev was illiterate, dark, scarred from smallpox, and looked nothing like the dead emperor. But he found an audience that did not care about resemblance. The Yaik Cossacks had recently been disciplined for mutiny. The Bashkirs of the southern Urals had been losing land to Russian colonists for a generation. The Old Believers, persecuted since the schism of the previous century, were waiting for a tsar who would restore the old faith. The serfs of the great estates wanted to stop being serfs. The factory workers of the Ural mining towns, bound to their furnaces in conditions worse than agricultural serfdom, wanted to stop being that. To all of them, Pugachev offered the same thing: a true tsar, returned, who would burn the nobles, expel the officials, and give the land back to those who worked it.

The rising spread with extraordinary speed. By the end of 1773 he was besieging Orenburg with an army of perhaps twenty-five thousand. By the summer of 1774 he had taken Kazan, the largest city east of Moscow, and burned most of it to the ground. The roads from the Volga to Saint Petersburg lay open. Nobles fled their estates. The capital, which had received the news with a kind of disbelief, began to panic.

What saved Catherine was the war. The Russo-Turkish war that had begun in 1768 ended that summer with the Treaty of Kuchuk-Kainardji, and the army that had defeated the Ottomans could now be sent against Pugachev. General Pyotr Panin and the young Alexander Suvorov took the field. The rebels, who had won against provincial garrisons, could not stand against professional troops. Pugachev's army was broken in August. He fled into the steppe, was betrayed by his own Cossack lieutenants, and was delivered to Suvorov in an iron cage.

He was taken to Moscow, interrogated, and executed in January 1775. The sentence specified quartering while alive; the executioner, by order or by mercy, cut off his head first. His body was burned. The villages that had supported him were burned too. The Yaik river was renamed the Ural to erase the memory of the Cossacks who had raised him up. For months afterward, gallows stood on rafts drifting down the Volga, bearing the bodies of hanged peasants past the riverside towns as a warning.

Catherine never spoke of Pugachev by name in her correspondence with the philosophes if she could avoid it. When she did, she called him the marquis de Pugachev, a sarcasm meant to reduce him to a curiosity. But the rebellion had frightened her, and it changed the shape of her rule. The provincial reform of 1775 multiplied the units of local government from twenty to fifty, brought the noble landlords into the administration of their own districts, and stationed garrisons in places that had previously had none. The Charter to the Nobility a decade later, which freed the nobles from compulsory service and confirmed their property in land and souls, was the other side of the same calculation. After Pugachev, Catherine ruled in partnership with her landlords. The serfs paid the bill.

Partitioning Poland, Annexing Crimea

To the west and to the south, Catherine's policy was simpler. She took what she could.

Poland in the eighteenth century was a republic of nobles with an elected king, a parliament that could be paralyzed by a single dissenting vote, and a foreign policy that had not been its own for decades. Catherine's former lover Stanislaw Poniatowski had been elected king in 1764 with Russian troops in the suburbs of Warsaw to ensure the result. He was intelligent, cultured, and entirely dependent on her. When Polish reformers tried to strengthen the state, Russian troops returned. When a Polish confederation rose against Russian interference in 1768, the war that followed dragged on for four years and drew in Prussia and Austria, both of whom had territorial appetites of their own.

The first partition, in 1772, was Frederick the Great's idea. Russia, Prussia and Austria each took a slice of Polish territory and forced the Polish parliament to ratify the seizure. Catherine took the eastern borderlands, mostly inhabited by Orthodox Belarusians and Ukrainians, and could present the annexation at home as a reunion of co-religionists. Prussia took the strip that connected Brandenburg to East Prussia. Austria took Galicia. Poland lost roughly a third of its land and a third of its people in a single year and signed the treaty acknowledging the loss.

The second partition came in 1793, after a brief Polish constitutional revival that Catherine treated as Jacobin contagion creeping toward her borders. Russia and Prussia helped themselves again, and Poland was reduced to a rump. The third, in 1795, finished the work. The remaining territory was divided among the three powers, the king abdicated, and Poland disappeared from the map of Europe. It would not reappear for one hundred and twenty-three years.

The southern campaign was older and ran on parallel tracks. The first Russo-Turkish war ended in 1774 with the Treaty of Kuchuk-Kainardji, which gave Russia a foothold on the Black Sea coast, the right to protect Orthodox Christians within the Ottoman Empire, and effective control over the Crimean Khanate, declared independent of Constantinople. Independence was a fiction. In 1783, with the khanate weakened by internal disputes that Russian agents had carefully encouraged, Catherine annexed Crimea outright. It was the first time a Muslim Tatar state, the last surviving fragment of the Golden Horde, had been absorbed into a Christian European empire.

The architect of the southern policy was Grigory Potemkin, Catherine's lover from the early 1770s and, by some accounts, her secret husband. He governed the new southern provinces, founded the cities of Kherson, Nikolayev, Sevastopol, and Yekaterinoslav, built the Black Sea Fleet from nothing, and in 1787 arranged the famous tour in which Catherine sailed down the Dnieper to inspect her new lands. The story of the painted villages erected for her benefit - the so-called Potemkin villages - is mostly a libel by a jealous Saxon diplomat, but the tour was a piece of imperial theatre on a scale Europe had not seen. The Austrian emperor, the Polish king and the British and French ambassadors travelled with her. A second war with the Ottomans followed almost immediately, and Russia won that one too.

By 1795 the empire had pushed its frontiers westward to the Niemen and southward to the Black Sea. It had absorbed millions of Catholic Poles, Uniate Ukrainians, Jewish townsmen, and Muslim Tatars, and now contained, for the first time, the largest Jewish population in the world, confined by Catherine's decrees to a Pale of Settlement that would shape Russian-Jewish life until the revolution.

The Limits of Enlightenment

In 1790 a minor official named Alexander Radishchev published a book called *A Journey from Saint Petersburg to Moscow*. It was a slim volume, modelled loosely on Sterne, that described an imagined journey between the two capitals and used each stop to denounce something: the corruption of officials, the venality of priests, the brutality of recruitment, and above all the condition of the serfs. Radishchev was a graduate of the Page Corps and the University of Leipzig, a customs official in good standing, and a reader of exactly the French philosophers Catherine had spent thirty years patronising. She read the book and wrote in the margin that the author was a rebel worse than Pugachev. He was arrested, sentenced to death, and then, by her clemency, exiled to Siberia.

The reaction was not a sudden change of heart. It had been building since 1789. The French Revolution had begun the previous summer, the Bastille had fallen, and the king to whom Catherine had once written admiringly was now a prisoner of his own subjects. Whatever she had thought the Enlightenment was for, it was not for that. She banned French books, recalled Russian students from Paris, broke off diplomatic relations after the regicide of 1793, and spent her last years denouncing the philosophes she had once corresponded with as poisoners of the public mind. The Nakaz was quietly forgotten. The young men who had been raised on her libraries discovered that the libraries had been closed.

The deeper limit had been visible all along. The Charter to the Nobility of 1785 had given the landlords a corporate identity, exemption from corporal punishment, security of property, and freedom from service. A parallel charter for the towns gave the urban estates a thinner version of the same privileges. There was no charter for the peasants. In the same decades during which Catherine wrote her letters to Voltaire and built her schools and bought her paintings, the legal condition of the serfs grew worse. They could be sold without land. They could be sent to Siberia by their masters without trial. They could not petition the empress directly - the right to do so had been removed in 1767, in the same year the Nakaz was read aloud to the Legislative Commission. By the end of her reign, roughly half the population of the empire was the personal property of the other half's smallest fraction.

She died in November 1796, struck by a stroke in her private apartments and lingering for a day and a half without regaining the power of speech. She was sixty-seven. Her son Paul, whom she had despised and from whom she had tried to exclude the succession in favour of her grandson Alexander, came in from his country estate and took the throne. One of his first acts was to have his father's remains exhumed from the monastery where they had lain since 1762 and reburied with full imperial honours beside Catherine's coffin. The two of them lay in state together: the murdered emperor and the wife who had outlived him by thirty-four years. The crowds filing past the catafalque were left to draw their own conclusions.

The crowds filed past the catafalque and drew their own conclusions. Catherine had ruled for thirty-four years and left her son a state that was larger, richer, and more cultured than the one she had seized, and an unfinished argument about what enlightenment in Russia could mean. Paul would not have long to rework that argument in his own image. Within five years the officers would walk into another palace bedroom, and another son would be waiting in another room of the same building, telling himself afterward that he had not known what they intended to do.

Chapter 8
1812: Napoleon at the Gates

Alexander I and the Liberal Tsar

He came to the throne with blood on the carpet. In March 1801, a group of officers walked into the bedroom of Paul I, demanded his abdication, and when he refused, strangled him. Alexander, his son, was in another room of the same palace, waiting. He had been told there would be a coup. He had not, he insisted afterward, been told there would be a murder. He spent the rest of his life arranging that fact in his mind.

He was twenty-three, tall, slightly deaf in one ear, charming in the way that men raised by tutors to be charming are charming. His grandmother Catherine had supervised his education personally, importing a Swiss republican named La Harpe to teach him about Rousseau and the rights of man. The result was a tsar who used the vocabulary of the Enlightenment with real fluency and who ruled, by inheritance, the most autocratic state in Europe. He felt the contradiction. He talked about it. For a few years at the start of his reign he seemed willing to do something about it.

There was talk of a constitution. There was a commission to draft new laws. Mikhail Speransky, the son of a village priest who had risen by sheer brain into the inner circles of government, produced detailed proposals for a separation of powers, an elected duma, a system of courts that would not simply do what the governor told them to do. Alexander read the proposals. He praised them. He let almost none of them become law. Speransky was eventually exiled to Nizhny Novgorod, in part to placate the noble families who had concluded that the priest's son intended to tax them.

What Alexander did do, in the first years, was loosen things. Censorship eased. Universities were founded at Kazan, Kharkov, and Saint Petersburg. Foreign books arrived again. Returning exiles found their estates restored. The serf question was discussed openly in private salons, sometimes with the tsar himself in the room, though the serfs themselves remained where they had always been, on the land, the property of the men in the salons.

Abroad, the picture was darker. Napoleon had crowned himself emperor in 1804. Russia joined the coalitions against him and was beaten, badly, at Austerlitz in 1805 and again at Friedland in 1807. After Friedland the two emperors met on a raft moored in the middle of the Niemen River at Tilsit, embraced for the benefit of their staffs, and signed a treaty. Alexander agreed to join the Continental System, Napoleon's economic blockade of Britain. He agreed because he had no choice. He went home and the Russian nobility, whose wealth depended on exporting grain and timber to British buyers, told him in plain terms what they thought of his choice.

For five years the alliance held in form and decayed in substance. Russian ports leaked British goods. French diplomats complained. Napoleon married an Austrian archduchess after Alexander declined to hand over his sister. Polish questions festered. By 1811 both emperors were preparing for a war neither one would say aloud he wanted. Alexander wrote to his sister Catherine that summer that he expected to fight and to lose the opening battles, and that his strategy, if it came to it, would be to retreat into the depth of his own country and let the winter do what his armies could not.

The Invasion

On the night of June 23, 1812, French sappers laid three pontoon bridges across the Niemen at Kovno. The next morning the army began to cross. It took them five days. There had never been an army like it in European history: somewhere between 450,000 and 600,000 men in the first wave, with reserves bringing the total over the campaign close to 680,000. Frenchmen, Poles, Italians, Saxons, Bavarians, Dutch, Swiss, Spaniards conscripted from occupied Spain, Portuguese who had been on the other side a year earlier, and detachments from every minor German principality that had attached itself to the empire. They called it the Grand Army. It was less a national force than a federation in uniform.

Napoleon himself crossed on the 24th. He rode along the riverbank in the gray dawn, his staff a few paces behind, and watched the columns move. He had given the campaign a name in advance: the Second Polish War. He expected it to last three weeks. The Russians would offer a battle near the border, he would beat them as he had beaten everyone else, Alexander would sue for peace at some convenient palace, and the Continental System would be patched back together. He had brought a court along to handle the diplomacy.

The Russians did not offer a battle. Their two main armies, one under Barclay de Tolly and one under Bagration, were separated by a hundred miles and outnumbered roughly two to one. They retreated. Barclay, who was minister of war as well as field commander, had spent two years preparing depots and stockpiles deeper in the country. Whether the long retreat was a coherent plan or a series of improvisations is a question historians have argued about ever since. What is clear is that the Russian armies kept moving east, declining engagement, and that the gap between them eventually closed near Smolensk in August.

The retreat infuriated almost everyone in Russia. Bagration, a Georgian prince of explosive temperament, wrote letters denouncing Barclay as a coward and probably a traitor on account of his Baltic German name. The court at Petersburg seethed. Moscow merchants demanded to know when someone would stand and fight. Soldiers burned villages as they pulled back so the French would find nothing to eat, and the peasants whose villages were being burned were not always informed in advance about the strategic rationale.

The French marched into the burned country. The heat that summer was extraordinary. Roads turned to dust that coated men and horses until they looked like statues. Then thunderstorms came and turned the dust to mud deep enough to swallow wheels. Horses began to die in numbers the army's veterinarians had never seen, partly from the work, partly from the green unripe rye they were eating because nothing else was available. By the time the Grand Army reached Smolensk in mid-August it had lost something close to a third of its strength without fighting a major battle. Stragglers, deserters, the sick, and the dead were strung out across five hundred miles of Lithuanian and Belorussian road.

At Smolensk there was finally a fight. The Russians defended the old walls for two days and then, in the night, withdrew through the burning city. Napoleon walked through the ruins the next morning. He was reported to have been quiet for a long time. One of his marshals, Caulaincourt, had been telling him since June that the war was a mistake and ought to be ended before winter. Napoleon listened and went on east.

In Petersburg, Alexander gave way at last to the pressure he had been resisting for two months. On August 29 he appointed Mikhail Kutuzov - a one-eyed veteran of sixty-seven who had been wounded twice in the head and was widely believed to be too old to ride a horse all day - as supreme commander. Kutuzov was Russian to the core, which the public required. He was also, as it turned out, one of the most patient commanders the war would produce. He arrived at the army, was greeted with cheers, and announced that he would give battle to save Moscow. Privately he had no intention of saving Moscow if saving it meant losing the army.

Borodino and the Burning of Moscow

Kutuzov chose the ground himself. Borodino was a village seventy miles west of Moscow, on the old Smolensk road, with a stream running across the front and a series of low ridges that could be fortified in the few days available. Russian peasants and soldiers dug earthworks through the first week of September. The largest of them, an open redoubt on the central rise, would be remembered as the Raevsky Battery. To the south, three smaller flèches anchored Bagration's wing.

On the morning of September 7 the two armies faced each other across the stream with roughly 130,000 men each and more than a thousand guns between them. The fighting began at dawn and lasted until dark. It was the bloodiest single day of the Napoleonic Wars and would remain the bloodiest day in European warfare until the First World War. Bagration's flèches changed hands seven times. Bagration himself was hit by a shell fragment that shattered his leg; he refused to leave the field until he had fainted from blood loss, and died three weeks later of gangrene. The Raevsky Battery was taken in the afternoon by a French cavalry charge that went in over a slope already covered with the dead.

By evening the Russian line had bent but not broken. The Grand Army had pushed forward perhaps a mile. Casualties on both sides came to somewhere around seventy thousand, possibly more; the exact figure has never been settled. Napoleon, suffering from a heavy cold and uncharacteristically indecisive, refused to commit his Imperial Guard for the final blow that some of his marshals were demanding. The Guard was his reserve, the last unbroken thing in the army, and he was eight hundred miles from France. He let it stand.

Kutuzov, in his report to Alexander written that night, claimed a victory. Two days later he ordered the army to retreat. At a council of war in the village of Fili, just outside Moscow, his generals argued for hours about whether to fight again in front of the city. Kutuzov listened and then said, in a sentence that would be quoted in every Russian schoolbook for the next two centuries, that the loss of Moscow was not the loss of Russia, but the loss of the army would be. He gave the order to abandon the capital.

On September 14 the French entered Moscow. They expected a delegation of nobles with keys on a velvet cushion. They found empty streets. The governor, Count Rostopchin, had organized an evacuation that emptied the city of nearly all its 270,000 inhabitants in a few days. Russian troops had marched out through one gate as the French marched in through another. Napoleon installed himself in the Kremlin.

That night the fires began. They spread fast through the wooden city, fanned by a hot wind, and by the second day large parts of Moscow were burning out of control. Whether the fires were set on Rostopchin's orders, by departing troops, by released prisoners, or by some combination of all three was disputed at the time and is disputed now. Rostopchin had removed the city's fire engines and pumps before leaving, which suggests he at least anticipated the result. By the time the wind dropped, two-thirds of Moscow was ash. The Kremlin survived. Napoleon had been forced to evacuate it temporarily and watched the city burn from a palace in the suburbs, reportedly muttering that the Russians were Scythians.

He stayed in Moscow for thirty-five days. He sent envoys to Alexander offering peace; Alexander did not reply. He sent envoys to Kutuzov, who was camped southwest of the city with an army that was growing daily as militia and reserves came in. Kutuzov received the envoys politely and sent them away with nothing. Each day the weather got colder. Each day the food situation in the burned city got worse. Each day Napoleon's marshals told him, with increasing directness, that the army had to leave.

The Grande Armée advanced nearly two thousand kilometers into Russia only to find an empire that could absorb catastrophe and still survive. The retreat from Moscow became one of history's most devastating military collapses.

The Long Retreat

On October 19 the Grand Army marched out of Moscow. It was already smaller than it had been when it entered: perhaps 100,000 effective troops, with a vast train of wagons loaded with loot from the city, including, famously, the gilded cross from the Ivan the Great Bell Tower, which Napoleon had ordered pried off as a trophy. The wagons would slow the army to a crawl on roads that were about to freeze.

Napoleon's intention was to retreat by a southern route through Kaluga, through country the war had not yet stripped, and then back to Smolensk along undamaged roads. Kutuzov blocked him. At Maloyaroslavets on October 24 the two armies fought a confused battle through a town that changed hands eight times in a single day. The French held the field at the end. Napoleon nevertheless turned the army north, back to the burned Smolensk road, the road they had come in on, the road that now had nothing on it at all.

The first hard frost came on November 5. The army had no winter clothing. Horses fell on the ice and could not get up; men cut steaks from them where they lay. Stragglers froze in the night and were found in the morning curled around the embers of fires that had gone out hours before. Cossack cavalry rode along the flanks of the column, picking off anyone who fell behind. Russian peasants, who had previously been the army's reluctant suppliers, now hunted French stragglers with pitchforks and scythes and a hatred that surprised the surviving officers when they wrote about it later.

Smolensk, when they reached it on November 9, had been so thoroughly stripped during the advance that the depot held food for only a few days. The army began to come apart in earnest. Discipline dissolved. Regiments that had been at full strength in June were down to a few dozen men carrying the eagle and walking together because walking alone was death.

The crossing of the Berezina River in the last week of November was where the catastrophe became legend. Russian armies converged from three directions on a French force trying to get its remaining troops, its camp followers, its wounded, and its plunder across a single river before the ice closed it. French engineers built two pontoon bridges in water already running with ice floes, working in shifts in the river itself; most of them died of exposure within days. Napoleon got the fighting core of his army across. Thousands of stragglers and civilians who tried to cross after the bridges were fired died in the water or on the eastern bank when the bridges were burned to prevent pursuit.

On December 5, at the town of Smorgon, Napoleon left the army. He climbed into a sleigh with Caulaincourt and rode for Paris, where, he had been informed, a coup attempt against him had nearly succeeded in his absence. He covered the distance in thirteen days. The army he left behind continued west under Murat. By the time the last French units crossed back over the Niemen in mid-December, fewer than one in ten of the men who had crossed it in June were still with the colors. The road behind them, all the way to Moscow, was lined with bodies that would still be visible when the snow melted in the spring.

From Paris to the Holy Alliance

Alexander did not stop at the border. His generals, including Kutuzov, argued for ending the war on Russian soil. The country was exhausted; the army had taken its own enormous casualties; the harvest was lost across a wide belt of the west; there was no obvious Russian interest in liberating Germany. Alexander overruled them. He had decided, somewhere in the months of waiting in Petersburg while his capital burned, that Napoleon had to be finished, and that he, Alexander, was the instrument by which God intended to do it. The religious vocabulary in his letters from this period is not decorative. He meant it.

The Russian army crossed into Poland in January 1813 and kept going. The Prussians, who had been French allies, switched sides in February. The Austrians joined the coalition in August. There was hard fighting through the summer and autumn, costing tens of thousands more lives, until a four-day battle outside Leipzig in October broke Napoleon's German army and forced him back across the Rhine. The allied armies followed in 1814. On March 31 of that year Alexander rode into Paris at the head of his Guard, on a gray horse, in a city that had not been entered by a foreign army in four centuries.

He behaved well in Paris. He restrained his troops, made a point of attending services at French churches, refused to take revenge on the city for the burning of Moscow, and treated the defeated French establishment with a courtesy that surprised everyone. Napoleon abdicated and was sent to Elba. The Bourbons came back. The map of Europe was redrawn at a congress in Vienna over the following winter, with Alexander present and arguing forcefully for a Polish kingdom under his own crown, which he eventually got in modified form.

At Vienna he began to talk about something larger than territory. He proposed an alliance of the Christian monarchs of Europe, bound not by interest but by the principles of the Gospel, pledged to treat their subjects as fathers and to treat each other as brothers. The document he drew up was signed in September 1815 by Alexander, the Austrian emperor Francis, and the Prussian king Frederick William. Metternich, the Austrian chancellor, called it a loud-sounding nothing and signed it because his master wanted him to. The British declined to join. The pope declined to join. The sultan was not asked.

The Holy Alliance, as the document came to be known, became something different from what its text suggested. Over the next decade it served as the framework for a series of congresses at which the conservative powers agreed to suppress revolutionary movements wherever they appeared - in Spain, in Italy, in the German states. The liberal tsar who had once read Rousseau with a Swiss tutor was now the senior partner in a coalition dedicated to ensuring that nobody else got to read Rousseau in dangerous places. Speransky, in exile, must have noted the symmetry.

Alexander himself grew stranger in the years after Paris. He became increasingly mystical, increasingly withdrawn, given to long conversations with a Baltic baroness who claimed prophetic gifts. He toured his empire restlessly. In 1825, on one such tour to the southern town of Taganrog, he caught a fever and died - or was said to have died. The rumor began almost immediately that the coffin had been empty, that Alexander had walked off into Siberia under another name to expiate the murder of his father, and that a holy hermit named Fyodor Kuzmich, who appeared in the Tomsk region some years later, was the former emperor of all the Russias. The rumor was never proven. It was never quite disproven either.

Whether the coffin at Taganrog was empty or full, Alexander left the throne the way he had taken it: in a fog of rumor and unfinished business. The succession that followed was botched in a way that gave a small group of officers their opening, and gave the new tsar his first lesson in what his reign would be about. The men who came out onto the Senate square that December morning believed they were defending a constitution. What they were actually doing was opening a long argument about whether reform in Russia could ever come from above, or would have to be torn from below.

Chapter 9
Decembrists, Tsars, and the Cage of Reform

The Decembrist Revolt

The square in front of the Senate building in St. Petersburg was iron-hard with cold on the morning of December 26, 1825. About three thousand soldiers stood in formation under officers who had told them they were defending the rightful heir to the throne. Most of the soldiers believed it. They shouted for Constantine, the elder brother of the new tsar, because their officers had taught them that "Constantine and Constitution" was the proper cry, and some of them thought Constitution was Constantine's wife.

Their officers knew better. They had been in Paris in 1814, riding behind Alexander I as the Russian army entered the city that had defied Napoleon. They had seen cafés, newspapers, parliaments, civilians who argued with their governments and lived to argue again the next morning. They had come home to a country where a landlord could sell a man away from his children, and where the tsar's word was the only law that mattered. For a decade they had met in secret societies, drafted constitutions in drawing rooms, debated whether Russia should become a constitutional monarchy or a republic, and what to do with the imperial family if it came to that.

Alexander I's death in November of 1825 caught them before they were ready. There followed three weeks of dynastic confusion: Constantine, the next in line, had quietly renounced the throne years earlier in favor of his younger brother Nicholas, but the renunciation had been kept secret. Soldiers and civil servants swore allegiance to Constantine; then, when the truth came out, they were told to swear again to Nicholas. The Decembrists, as they would later be called, saw their opening in this second oath. They would refuse it, march their regiments to the Senate, and force the new government to accept a constitution.

What followed was less a revolt than a long, freezing hesitation. The officers' chosen "dictator," Prince Sergei Trubetskoy, never came to the square. Nicholas, twenty-nine years old and uncertain whether the garrison would obey him, sent emissaries to plead with the rebels. One of them, the military governor of St. Petersburg, was shot from his horse by a Decembrist officer named Kakhovsky. The standoff lasted hours. Crowds gathered. A pale winter sun moved across the sky and began to set.

Nicholas ordered the artillery to load with grapeshot. The first rounds went over the rebels' heads. The next did not. Soldiers broke and ran across the frozen Neva, where more cannon fire cracked the ice beneath them. By evening the square was empty except for bodies and bloodied snow.

The investigation that followed was meticulous, and Nicholas personally interrogated many of the prisoners. Five of the leaders were hanged - Pestel, Ryleyev, Kakhovsky, Bestuzhev-Ryumin, Muravyov-Apostol - in a botched execution where the ropes of three of them broke and they had to be hauled up and hanged a second time. More than a hundred others were sent to Siberia. Some of their wives followed them, abandoning titles and estates to live in log houses near the silver mines, and these women became the first heroines of the Russian revolutionary imagination.

The Decembrists had failed at almost everything. Their plot was disorganized, their leaders absent, their soldiers misled. But they were officers of noble birth - the tsar's own class - and they had drawn swords against him. That fact could not be unmade. For the rest of the century, every Russian who thought seriously about politics had to reckon with what had happened in the Senate Square, and what it meant that the men who tried to free Russia had been hanged at dawn by a tsar who slept badly afterward.

Nicholas I: Orthodoxy, Autocracy, Nationality

Nicholas was a man of parade grounds. He liked uniforms, geometry, punctuality, and the sound of boots striking stone in unison. He distrusted lawyers, professors, and anyone who used the word "progress" without irony. He had come to the throne over the bodies of his own officers, and he never forgot it.

For thirty years he ruled Russia as if it were a regiment that needed constant inspection. He created the Third Section of His Imperial Majesty's Own Chancellery, a political police that read private correspondence, watched salons, and kept files on the country's writers. He doubled the size of the bureaucracy and personally signed off on decisions that in any other European state would have been left to a clerk. He believed that if he stopped paying attention for even a moment, the empire would slip into the chaos he had glimpsed in the Senate Square.

His official ideology was named by his education minister, Count Sergei Uvarov, in a phrase that would be repeated until it became a kind of catechism: Orthodoxy, Autocracy, Nationality. The Orthodox Church was the moral foundation of the people. The autocrat was the only legitimate political authority. The Russian nation, with its peasant piety and its distrust of Western abstraction, was different in essence from the nations of Europe and must not be polluted by their constitutional experiments. The formula had the advantage of explaining why nothing needed to change.

Censorship grew thick. Books had to pass through committees that could reject them for a sentence, a phrase, a single noun. Universities were placed under the eye of the police, the number of students capped, the curriculum trimmed of philosophy. Foreign travel was restricted; passports for young men became hard to obtain after the revolutions of 1848 swept across Europe and left every monarch on the continent badly shaken. Nicholas watched those revolutions with the satisfaction of a man whose worst opinions about humankind have been confirmed.

Beneath the surface, a generation of writers and thinkers was forming itself in opposition to him, or in argument with him, or in private despair. Pushkin wrote within the limits the tsar allowed him, and sometimes outside them, and died in a duel that the government regarded with relief. Gogol published *Dead Souls*, a novel about a man buying the legal title to deceased serfs, and the censors did not quite understand what they were reading. A circle of young men in Moscow argued for nights on end about whether Russia's destiny was Western or its own; the Slavophiles and the Westernizers, as they came to be called, disagreed about everything except that the country they lived in could not go on as it was.

The most famous of Nicholas's victims was a junior army engineer named Fyodor Dostoevsky, arrested in 1849 for belonging to a discussion circle that read banned books aloud. He was sentenced to death, marched out to a parade ground in his shirt, and made to stand before the firing squad while the tsar's pardon, prepared in advance for theatrical effect, was read out at the last moment. Then he was sent to Siberia for four years of hard labor. He came back a different writer.

Serfdom remained the central fact of Russian life. Roughly half the empire's population belonged either to private landowners or to the state, and could be bought, mortgaged, transferred, or punished at the owner's discretion. Nicholas detested serfdom and said so privately. He commissioned no fewer than nine secret committees to study what might be done about it. None of them did anything. The tsar who had crushed his officers for trying to change Russia could not bring himself to change it himself. What finally moved the question was not a committee. It was a war.

The Crimean War and Imperial Humiliation

The war began, as wars often do, over something small. In 1853 a dispute over which Christian clergy should hold the keys to certain churches in the Holy Land - a Catholic monk's quarrel with an Orthodox priest, with the French and the Russians behind them - escalated into a Russian ultimatum to the Ottoman Empire. Nicholas believed the Ottomans were a dying state ripe for partition. He believed Austria, whose throne he had personally helped to save during the revolutions of 1848, would stand with him out of gratitude. He believed Britain and France would not act in concert. He was wrong on every count.

By the spring of 1854, Russia was at war with the Ottomans, the British, the French, and eventually the Kingdom of Sardinia. Austria stood neutral in a way that felt to Nicholas like betrayal and which probably hastened his death. The fighting took place across several theaters - in the Caucasus, in the Baltic, even in the far Pacific, where a small Anglo-French squadron attacked Petropavlovsk - but the war is remembered by the name of the peninsula where its decisive campaign unfolded.

The allied armies landed in the Crimea in September 1854 and laid siege to the great Russian naval base at Sevastopol. The siege lasted almost a year. Russian soldiers fought with extraordinary courage from earthworks designed by a brilliant military engineer named Eduard Totleben, and died in numbers that no one in St. Petersburg could quite believe. They died of allied shells and they died of typhus and dysentery and cold and hunger and the sheer inadequacy of a supply system that could not get them food and bandages from a country that had almost no railways.

That was the heart of the humiliation. The British arrived with steamships and rifled muskets and a telegraph line that ran from London to a tent outside Sevastopol. They had a press that printed dispatches from the front within weeks, and a nurse named Florence Nightingale who reorganized the field hospitals when the dispatches revealed how bad they were. The Russians fought with smoothbore muskets that could not match the range of the allied rifles. They moved their reinforcements south on dirt roads, in carts pulled by oxen, sometimes for two months from the recruiting depots. By the time the men arrived they were exhausted and the war had moved on.

Sevastopol fell in September 1855. By then Nicholas was dead - he had caught a cold in February, refused to take care of himself, and slipped into a pneumonia from which he did not recover. His last conversation with his son, the future Alexander II, was reportedly bleak. "I am handing you my command, but not in the order I would have wished," he is said to have whispered, "and I leave you with much trouble and worry."

The Treaty of Paris in 1856 stripped Russia of its right to maintain a navy in the Black Sea and ended its claim to act as protector of the Ottoman Empire's Orthodox Christians. Materially, the losses could have been worse. Symbolically, they were catastrophic. Russia had presented itself for forty years as the gendarme of Europe, the power that had broken Napoleon and stabilized the continent. Now a few divisions of British and French infantry, fighting at the end of a supply line that stretched across a sea, had defeated the Russian army on its own soil.

Every educated Russian drew the same conclusion, though they drew it in different words. The country was not what its rulers said it was. Its peasant soldiers were brave and its officers were not all incompetent, but its economy could not equip an army, its bureaucracy could not move one, and its institutions could not learn from defeat. Something at the foundation would have to be rebuilt. The new tsar understood this. He had been raised under his father's discipline and shared many of his father's instincts, but he had also watched the war from inside the government and had no illusions about what serfdom and stagnation had cost. In a famous speech to the nobility of Moscow in 1856 he told them plainly that it was better to abolish serfdom from above than to wait for it to abolish itself from below.

Alexander II and the Emancipation of the Serfs

The drafting took five years. Committees of officials and landowners argued through every winter of the late 1850s about questions that had no clean answers. If the serfs were freed, would they get land? If they got land, who would pay the landlords for it? If the landlords were compensated, who would pay them - the state, the peasants, or some combination? If the peasants paid, over how many years, and at what interest? What would prevent them from drifting into the cities, or refusing to work, or simply walking off the estates where their grandparents had been buried?

The manifesto Alexander signed on February 19, 1861, ran to hundreds of pages of attached statutes. It declared that some twenty-three million privately owned serfs were now free persons with the right to marry, own property, and bring suit in court. It granted them a portion of the land they had worked - usually a smaller portion than they had been farming, and usually the worse soil. It required them to pay redemption dues to the state, which had compensated the landlords, over a period of forty-nine years. And it bound them, in most cases, not to themselves as individuals but to the village commune, the *mir*, which held the land collectively and could not be dissolved without the agreement of its members.

The reaction in the villages was confusion, sometimes anger. Many peasants had imagined freedom as the gift of all the land they worked, without payment. The actual settlement, in which they were told they owed money for fields they had always considered their own, struck them as a trick. In some places they refused to believe the manifesto was authentic and assumed the real one, the tsar's true word, was being hidden from them by local officials. There were riots. Troops were sent. The most serious clashes left dozens dead.

Still, something fundamental had changed. A person could no longer be sold. A landlord could no longer have his peasant flogged for the look on his face. The legal category that had defined

Russian society for centuries was gone, and with it the moral basis of the old regime. Alexander pressed on with a series of further reforms that, taken together, amounted to the most ambitious program of modernization any Russian government had attempted.

The judicial reform of 1864 created independent courts, trial by jury for serious criminal cases, and a bar of professional defense lawyers. For the first time in Russian history a peasant and a prince could appear before the same judge under the same procedure. The *zemstvo* reform of the same year created elected councils at the district and provincial level, with responsibility for schools, roads, hospitals, and famine relief. The councils were dominated by the gentry but included peasant representatives, and they produced, over the following decades, a thin but real layer of practical public service - the country doctors and rural teachers who would appear in so much late Russian fiction. Military service was reformed in 1874, with conscription extended to all classes and the term of service cut from twenty-five years to six. Censorship was relaxed. Universities were given a measure of autonomy.

None of this was a constitution. Alexander never seriously considered limiting his own authority, and the press that flourished briefly under the new rules could still be shut down at the tsar's pleasure. But the cumulative effect of the reforms was to introduce, into a system designed to resist them, the elements of a modern state: independent courts, local self-government, an army of citizens rather than serfs, a public sphere in which arguments could be made out loud.

The men and women who made arguments out loud were not, on the whole, grateful. The generation that came of age in the 1860s read Chernyshevsky and Bakunin and began to call itself the intelligentsia, a Russian word that would soon enter every European language. Some of them went "to the people" in the summer of 1874, walking out into the villages dressed as peasants to preach socialism, and discovered that the peasants distrusted them and sometimes turned them in to the police. Others drew the conclusion that the people could not be reached by argument and would have to be liberated by force.

By the late 1870s a group calling itself People's Will had decided that the only target worth striking was the tsar himself. They tried to blow up his train. They tried to blow up his dining room in the Winter Palace, killing eleven soldiers in the basement guardroom while the tsar dined upstairs with a foreign prince who happened to be late. They were patient and ingenious and unlucky. On March 1, 1881, on the embankment of the Catherine Canal in St. Petersburg, they were lucky at last. A bomb thrown under his carriage wounded a Cossack and his coachman. Alexander stepped out, against his guards' advice, to see to the wounded. A second bomb tore off his legs. He was carried to the Winter Palace and died there within the hour.

Reform and Reaction

His son was a large, bearded, physically powerful man who had watched his father bleed out on a sofa in the Winter Palace. Alexander III drew his conclusion immediately and never revised it: reform had caused this. The judicial system that allowed defense lawyers to make speeches, the universities that produced students who read Bakunin, the press that printed criticism of the throne - all of it had created the people who killed his father. A draft proposal for a kind of consultative assembly, which the dying tsar had approved that very morning, was shelved within weeks.

The new reign began with hangings. Five of the conspirators, including a young woman named Sofia Perovskaya who had given the signal on the canal embankment, were executed in public. Then the screws began to turn on everything else. The Statute on Measures for the Preservation of State Order, issued in August 1881, gave provincial governors the power to declare states of emergency, ban gatherings, close newspapers, and exile suspects without trial. It was meant as a temporary measure. It remained in force, in one form or another, until the end of the empire.

The autonomy of universities was rolled back. Tuition was raised to keep the children of the lower classes out. The *zemstvo* councils were placed under tighter supervision by appointed officials called land captains, who could overrule peasant courts and personally order corporal punishment. The press was again throttled. A new chief procurator of the Holy Synod, Konstantin Pobedonostsev, who had been Alexander III's tutor and remained his closest adviser, set himself against everything that smelled of liberalism, parliamentarism, or religious tolerance. He believed parliaments were "the great lie of our time" and said so in writing.

Pobedonostsev's policy toward the empire's minorities followed from his theology. Russification was tightened in the Baltic provinces, in Poland, in Ukraine, where the use of the Ukrainian language in print had already been restricted under Alexander II and was now restricted further. Jews, who lived mostly in the Pale of Settlement in the empire's western borderlands, became the targets of a wave of pogroms in 1881 and 1882 that the government did little to prevent and sometimes quietly encouraged. The May Laws of 1882 restricted where Jews could live, what trades they could enter, and how many of their children could attend the empire's schools and universities. Emigration began on a scale that would, within a generation, transform Jewish communities from New York to Buenos Aires.

Industrial Russia, meanwhile, was beginning to move. Under the finance ministers of the 1880s and 1890s the empire built railways at a pace that would have astonished the men who fought the Crimean War. The Trans-Siberian was begun in 1891. Factories rose in St. Petersburg, in Moscow, in the Donbas coalfields, in the oil towns around Baku. A working class was forming in the cities, drawn from the same villages whose grandfathers had been emancipated thirty years earlier, and it was already restive. The reforms that the throne had refused to extend were being produced anyway, by capital and steam, in places the throne could not directly see.

Alexander III died of kidney disease in 1894, at the age of forty-nine, leaving his throne to his eldest son - a slight, courteous, gray-eyed young man named Nicholas who had never expected to rule so soon, who had been given almost no preparation for the work, and who privately confessed to a cousin in the days after his father's death that he did not know what to do or how to talk to ministers. He was twenty-six. The country he had inherited contained a hundred and thirty million people, a half-built industrial economy, a peasantry still paying redemption dues on land it had never accepted as anything but its own, an intelligentsia that had begun to organize itself into political parties, and a secret police that knew most of their names.

The lamps were still burning, late into the winter nights, in apartments in St. Petersburg and Geneva and Zurich, where small groups of men and women argued about how the next attempt would be made.

The lamps burning late in apartments in Petersburg and Geneva and Zurich were lit by people who had decided that the cage of reform was not going to be opened by the men who held the keys. Some of them still believed in books, in argument, in the slow work of persuading peasants and students and factory hands. Others had begun to believe in something else. The next attempt would not be made by officers on a parade square. It would be made by chemists in basements, by students in peasant boots, and by men and women who had stopped expecting the tsar to be argued with.

Chapter 10
Bombs and Books: The Revolutionary Underground

Going to the People

In the summer of 1874, several thousand young Russians put on peasant boots and walked out of the cities. Some carried medical kits. Some carried books. A few carried pamphlets they had printed in basements, explaining to villagers in plain Russian that the land they tilled was theirs by right and that the Tsar was not their father but their jailer.

They called what they were doing "going to the people." They were students, mostly - the children of officials and minor nobles and priests - and they had decided that the answer to Russia's misery lay not in Petersburg drawing rooms but in the wooden villages where four out of five Russians lived. They believed the peasant commune, the *obshchina*, was already a kind of socialism in embryo. All it needed was to be awakened.

The peasants, for the most part, turned them in to the police.

This was not what the populists had expected. They had imagined being received as brothers. Instead they were eyed with suspicion, fed sometimes, lectured at occasionally about the goodness of the Tsar, and then handed over to the local constable. By the autumn the prisons were filling with idealists who had not even managed to deliver their pamphlets. The great trials of the late 1870s - the Trial of the 50, the Trial of the 193 - paraded these young men and women through the courts and into Siberian exile.

The shock of failure changed everything. If the people would not rise on their own, then the people would have to be helped. And if peaceful agitation only put its preachers in chains, then what was left was force.

The reforms of Alexander II hung over all of this like an unkept promise. In 1861 he had freed the serfs - more than twenty million of them - in a stroke that no other European monarch had matched. But the freedom came with conditions that strangled it. The peasants received land, but they had to pay for it over forty-nine years, at prices set above the market. They remained tied to the commune, which collected the redemption payments and bound them to the village as firmly as the old landlord ever had. The reform that was supposed to open Russia produced, in the countryside, a sullen kind of hunger.

The students who walked into the villages in 1874 had grown up reading about that emancipation as a triumph. What they found was something else: hut after hut of people who could not read the pamphlets being pressed on them, who suspected the strangers of being agents of the landlords, and who, when winter came, would still owe the state for the soil under their feet.

Out of this disappointment, a harder movement crystallized. In 1879, in a forest near Voronezh, the loose populist network *Zemlya i Volya* - Land and Liberty - split in two. One faction wanted to keep up patient propaganda. The other had decided that the autocracy itself was the obstacle, and that the autocracy could be removed by killing the autocrat. They took the name *Narodnaya Volya*, the People's Will. They were a few dozen people. They believed they could overthrow an empire of a hundred million by an act of will, and a sufficient quantity of nitroglycerin.

Marx and Engels, watching from London, were intrigued. The Russian populists were not orthodox socialists by their lights, but they were doing something. The two old men corresponded with them, encouraged them, and waited to see what would happen if you put a bomb under the Romanov throne.

The People's Will gave Alexander II a death sentence in August 1879. They issued it as if they were a court. Then they spent eighteen months trying to carry it out.

They tried to mine the railway line he traveled on from the Crimea. The first attempt failed because the train carrying him had been switched to a different route. The second attempt exploded under the wrong train. In February 1880, a carpenter named Stepan Khalturin, who had spent months working inside the Winter Palace as a craftsman while smuggling dynamite into his quarters one slab at a time, detonated his charge in a basement directly beneath the dining room. Eleven soldiers of the guard were killed. Thirty more were wounded. The Tsar, delayed by the late arrival of a guest, was not in the room.

By the winter of 1881 the conspirators were running out of money and people. Most of the original executive committee was in prison. Those still at liberty knew they had weeks, perhaps days, before the police closed in. They decided to make one more attempt.

On the morning of Sunday, March 1, 1881, four young men took up positions along the route Alexander would take back from a military parade. Each carried a small bomb wrapped in newspaper. The lead conspirator, Sofia Perovskaya - the daughter of a former governor of Saint Petersburg - signaled to them with a wave of her handkerchief.

The first bomb, thrown by a student named Rysakov, struck the Tsar's armored carriage. It killed a Cossack outrider and a butcher's boy who happened to be in the street. The Tsar himself, miraculously, climbed out unhurt. He stood in the snow, surveying the wreckage, and insisted on going to look at the wounded boy. An officer urged him to leave at once. Alexander refused.

A second bomber, Ignaty Grinevitsky, stepped out of the crowd and threw his bomb at the Tsar's feet. The blast tore Alexander's legs apart. Grinevitsky himself was mortally wounded; he died that evening without giving his name. The Tsar was carried back to the Winter Palace on a sledge, leaving a trail of blood through the corridors. He died in the same study where, that morning, he had been preparing to sign a document creating an elected consultative assembly - a tentative first step, his ministers hoped, toward something like a constitution.

His son Alexander III tore the document up.

The People's Will believed that the death of the Tsar would set off a national rising - that the peasants, freed from the spell of the autocrat, would pour into the streets. Nothing of the sort happened. The peasants in many villages reportedly assumed the nobles had killed the Tsar in revenge for the emancipation. In the capital, crowds gathered to pray for the dead emperor and to curse his murderers.

Within weeks, the police had most of the conspirators. Five of them, including Perovskaya, were hanged in public on a scaffold in Semenovsky Square on April 3. She was the first woman in Russia to be executed for a political crime. She was twenty-seven.

The new Tsar issued a manifesto in late April reaffirming the unshakable principle of autocracy. The censorship was tightened. The universities were brought under closer control. A new political police, the Okhrana, was created to hunt revolutionaries with methods more systematic than anything the empire had used before. The People's Will, as an organization, disintegrated within two years. Its survivors went to the gallows, to Siberia, or into exile in Switzerland, where they had time to think about what had gone wrong - and one of the things they began to think about was Karl Marx.

Industrialization and a New Working Class

While the conspirators were planning their bombs, Russia was changing under their feet in a way none of them had quite reckoned with. The country the populists had imagined - the eternal village, the commune, the peasant as the moral basis of any future society - was beginning to be overtaken by something else entirely.

It started slowly. The Moscow textile mills had been turning out cotton since the 1840s. After the emancipation, the rural overpopulation that the redemption payments helped create began to push hungry men into the cities looking for work. In the 1880s, under the finance ministers Nikolai Bunge and Ivan Vyshnegradsky, and then with extraordinary acceleration under Sergei Witte in the 1890s, the state poured money and policy into building railroads, steel mills, oil fields, and coal mines.

The Trans-Siberian Railway was begun in 1891. The Baku oil fields, in what is now Azerbaijan, were producing more crude by the late 1890s than the United States. The Donbas in eastern Ukraine sprouted iron and coal works, much of the capital French and Belgian. Saint Petersburg's southern suburbs filled with engineering plants. The Putilov works alone employed more than twelve thousand men by the turn of the century.

This was a state-driven industrial revolution, not a private one. Witte's strategy depended on foreign loans, high tariffs to protect new factories, and a gold standard introduced in 1897 to make the ruble attractive to investors in Paris and Berlin. The peasantry paid for it. Grain was exported even in years of poor harvest to service the foreign debt. The famine of 1891-92, which killed somewhere between 375,000 and half a million people, happened against a backdrop of grain ships sailing out of Odessa.

The cities filled up. By 1900 Saint Petersburg had a million and a half inhabitants; Moscow nearly as many. Around the new factories, on the edges of the old capitals, grew districts that no one had planned and few visited: wooden barracks, mud streets, a single privy for hundreds of workers, tuberculosis everywhere. The factory workday was eleven and a half hours, twelve in some industries, and many of the workers were children. A law of 1882 forbade the employment of children under twelve. It was widely ignored.

The people in these barracks were peasants, technically. Most had villages they still belonged to legally, wives and parents back in the countryside to whom they sent money when they could. But their children were growing up in the cities, learning to read at workplace literacy circles, comparing wages with one another. They were not the silent, devout figures the populists had hoped to awaken in the villages. They were something newer and harder to predict.

Strikes began in the textile mills. A famous one at the Morozov mill at Orekhovo-Zuyevo in 1885 brought eleven thousand workers out and ended with troops, arrests, and a trial at which the workers' grievances were aired so publicly that the government was embarrassed into passing factory legislation the following year. There were strikes in the Saint Petersburg metal trades in the early 1890s, and a great strike of textile workers in 1896 and 1897 that paralyzed the capital's mills and forced through a law setting the workday at eleven and a half hours.

For a small group of intellectuals watching from emigration in Geneva and Zurich, this was the thing they had been waiting for. The populists had been wrong, they argued, not because they had wanted revolution but because they had looked for it in the wrong place. The peasantry was not the revolutionary class - if anything, it was a brake on history. The revolution would come from the men in the Putilov works and the women in the Moscow cotton mills, because Russia was, despite everything, finally beginning to look like the kind of country Marx had described. The strikes were proof. The barracks were proof. The cholera that swept through the workers' districts every few summers was proof. There was now, in the empire of the Tsars, a proletariat. The question was what to do with it.

Marxism Arrives in Russia

The first Russian Marxists were former populists who had read their way out of populism. The central figure was Georgy Plekhanov, who as a young man had marched with Land and Liberty and helped lead a famous demonstration outside the Kazan Cathedral in 1876. He had refused to follow the majority into terrorism in 1879, gone into exile in 1880, and in Switzerland had begun reading Marx.

In 1883, with Vera Zasulich, Pavel Axelrod, and a few others, Plekhanov founded the Emancipation of Labor group in Geneva. They were five or six people in a foreign city, writing pamphlets in Russian to be smuggled across the border. They were also, in retrospect, the beginning of Russian social democracy.

Zasulich was the most famous of them. In 1878 she had walked into the office of the governor of Saint Petersburg, General Trepov, and shot him at close range for ordering the flogging of a political prisoner. She had been tried by jury and acquitted, to the astonishment of Europe, and spirited out of the country before the government could rearrest her. She was a figure of the populist heroic tradition. By the early 1880s she had concluded that the heroic tradition had failed, and she spent the rest of her life writing about class struggle.

The Emancipation of Labor group made two arguments, and they spent twenty years making them. The first was that Russia was now a capitalist country, whether the populists wanted to admit it or not, and that no amount of nostalgia for the peasant commune was going to put the railroads back in their boxes. The second was that the working class - not the peasantry and not a heroic conspiratorial elite - would make the Russian revolution.

In 1883 the Russian working class was perhaps a million people in a population of more than a hundred million. The peasants still vastly outnumbered them. The populist tradition still held the imagination of most Russian radicals, and the surviving fragments of the People's Will still believed in the bomb. What changed the argument was the strikes. As the factory districts filled and the disputes multiplied, the Marxist analysis began to look less like a doctrinaire borrowing from Germany and more like a description of what was happening on the ground in Ivanovo-Voznesensk. Marx himself, late in life, had wondered whether Russia might skip the capitalist stage and pass directly from the commune to socialism; he had written sympathetically to Russian populists about the possibility. By the 1890s his Russian followers had decided he had been too generous. There would be no shortcut.

Plekhanov sent his pamphlets back into Russia, where small groups of students and workers read them in study circles in factory districts. In 1895 a young lawyer from Simbirsk, recently arrived in Saint Petersburg, helped pull together one of those circles into something he called the League of Struggle for the Emancipation of the Working Class. He was arrested within months and sent to Siberia. His name was Vladimir Ulyanov. He had taken to signing his political writings, for reasons of secrecy, with a pseudonym he formed from the name of the river Lena.

In 1898 a handful of delegates from study circles around the empire met in Minsk and declared themselves the Russian Social Democratic Labor Party. The police arrested most of them within weeks. The party existed mostly on paper. But it existed.

The Golden Age of Russian Literature

While the bombers were laying their mines and the Marxists were arguing about the peasantry, another set of Russians was at work on what would turn out to be the most enduring product of the nineteenth century - a literature that, within a generation, the rest of the world would read with the kind of attention it had once given to the Greeks.

Leo Tolstoy was forty-one when he began *War and Peace* and fifty when he finished *Anna Karenina*. By the 1880s he was living on his estate at Yasnaya Polyana, dressed in peasant clothes, writing tracts against private property, the church, the state, and the eating of meat. He had become an institution unto himself. The government feared excommunicating him, then excommunicated him anyway in 1901, and discovered that this only made him more popular. Pilgrims came to his door. Foreign journalists came. Peasants came, asking for advice on disputes with their landlords. He answered the mail himself.

Fyodor Dostoevsky had taken a different road to the same place. Arrested in 1849 for belonging to a discussion circle of liberal intellectuals, he had been marched out to be shot, then reprieved on the scaffold and sent to a Siberian penal colony for four years, followed by army service. He came back changed. The novels he wrote in the 1860s and 1870s - *Crime and Punishment, The Idiot, Demons, The Brothers Karamazov* - took the questions the revolutionaries were asking and put them inside the minds of murderers, saints, and epileptics. *Demons*, published in 1872, was a direct attack on the revolutionary underground, based on a real case in which a small Nechayev cell had killed one of its own members to bind the rest in blood. Dostoevsky thought he saw, in the young men with bombs, something genuinely demonic. He died in January 1881, six weeks before the People's Will killed the Tsar. Tolstoy outlived him by nearly thirty years. The two never met.

Around these two towered a generation: Ivan Turgenev, whose *Fathers and Sons* had coined the word *nihilist* as a Russian political category in 1862; Nikolai Leskov, with his strange tales of provincial saints and swindlers; the poet Fyodor Tyutchev; the satirist Mikhail Saltykov-Shchedrin. By the 1890s a younger group was coming up. Anton Chekhov, who had begun as a writer of humorous sketches to pay for medical school, was filling the new theaters with plays in which almost nothing seemed to happen and everything was at stake. Maxim Gorky, born Alexei Peshkov in 1868, had grown up in the underclass the others mostly wrote about from above; he was self-taught, had worked as a baker and a dockhand, and was about to publish stories from the tramping life that would make him famous across Europe.

What linked them was an assumption that literature was the one place in Russian life where the truth could be told. The newspapers were censored. The universities were watched. The Duma did not yet exist. But a novel, if it was long and serious enough, could pass through the censors and into the hands of readers who would argue about it for the next year. Dostoevsky's *Brothers Karamazov* and Tolstoy's *What Is to Be Done* were not just books. They were the public sphere.

The young people who were learning, in the 1880s and 1890s, to build bombs and to translate Marx had grown up on these books. They could quote Pushkin. They argued about whether Bazarov in *Fathers and Sons* was a hero or a warning. They believed, with an intensity that their German and French equivalents found startling, that a question raised in a novel was a question that demanded an answer in life.

In a basement in Geneva in 1900, a small group of exiles began typesetting a new newspaper. They printed it on thin paper so that it could be smuggled across the border in the linings of suitcases. They called it *Iskra*, the Spark, after a line from a poem the Decembrists had written in their Siberian exile seventy years earlier. *From a spark a flame will be kindled.*

From a spark a flame will be kindled. The line had been written by Decembrists in Siberia, picked up by exiles in Geneva, and printed on paper thin enough to smuggle in a suitcase lining. The men and women who typeset Iskra in 1900 were not yet a government in waiting, and most of them would have laughed at the suggestion. But the country they were writing for was changing faster than the throne above it could absorb. Within five years the strikes and the soldiers and the petitions would come together in a way that no one, in the basement or the Winter Palace, had quite anticipated.

Chapter 11
1905: Russia's First Revolution

The Last Tsar

He kept a diary in a small, careful hand, and the entries are almost unbearable to read in hindsight. The weather. The walks. The shooting of crows in the park at Tsarskoe Selo. A dinner with Mama. A long talk with Alix. The man writing was the autocrat of all the Russias, ruler of a sixth of the earth's surface and a hundred and thirty million subjects, and the strongest impression his private writing leaves is of a country gentleman who would have preferred to be left alone.

Nicholas II had come to the throne in 1894 at the age of twenty-six, sincerely believing that he was not ready and would never be ready. His father, Alexander III, had been a bear of a man who could bend silver rubles in his fingers and who treated his heir as a boy long after the boy was a grown officer. Nicholas inherited his father's politics without his father's authority. He believed, as a matter of religious conviction, that he had been anointed by God to hand on the autocracy intact to his own son. He also believed, as a matter of temperament, that bureaucrats were tiresome, that ministers exaggerated, and that the simple Russian people loved their tsar.

The country he ruled was changing faster than his diary could register. The emancipation of the serfs in 1861 had freed forty million peasants without giving them enough land to live on. Workshops in Moscow and the new factories of St. Petersburg, Lodz, and Baku were absorbing a generation of peasant sons who slept twelve to a room and worked eleven-hour shifts. The railways had quadrupled in length. Foreign capital, much of it French, was pouring into mines and metalworks. A literate urban class was reading newspapers Nicholas did not read and arguing about ideas he did not entertain.

His wife, Alexandra, a German princess who had become more Russian than the Russians and more Orthodox than the Orthodox, reinforced every instinct toward isolation. She disliked the court, distrusted ministers, and adored her husband with a possessive intensity that left little room for political advice from anyone else. When their first four children turned out to be daughters, the strain of waiting for an heir tightened the small circle around the imperial family still further. The son finally arrived in 1904, named Alexei after the gentle tsar of the seventeenth century, and within weeks it was clear he had hemophilia. The secret would shape Russian politics for the next thirteen years.

None of this excused the way Nicholas governed, but it explains the texture of it. He met with his ministers one at a time, agreed with whoever had spoken to him most recently, and then quietly undid their decisions when the next minister came in. He hated to fire anyone face-to-face and so dismissed officials by letter, often while assuring them in conversation that he held them in the highest regard. The result, by 1903, was a government in which no one knew who had been overruled and no one trusted the man at the top to mean what he said.

It was into this brittle structure that the first blow fell, and it came from a place almost no one in Petersburg had bothered to study on a map.

Defeat by Japan

The trouble began over timber and railways. Russian speculators with court connections had taken concessions on the Yalu River in Korea; Russian troops, sent during the Boxer Rebellion, had stayed on in Manchuria long after the other powers withdrew. Port Arthur, leased from China in 1898, gave Russia a warm-water harbor on the Pacific and a forward base for further pressure on Korea. The Japanese government, which had spent thirty years reorganizing itself along European lines specifically to avoid being treated as China was being treated, asked repeatedly for negotiations. The Russian Foreign Ministry, run by men who referred to the Japanese as monkeys, did not bother to answer the last telegram.

On the night of February 8, 1904, Japanese torpedo boats slipped into the roadstead at Port Arthur and crippled three Russian warships at anchor. The declaration of war followed the attack. In St. Petersburg the news was greeted with a kind of cheerful contempt. Interior Minister Vyacheslav Plehve was reported to have said that what Russia needed was a small victorious war to stem the tide of revolution. He would be assassinated by a bomb six months later, before any victory could be arranged.

The war was not small and there was no victory. The Russian Pacific Squadron, bottled up in Port Arthur, was sunk in detail through the spring and summer. A relief army under General Kuropatkin, transported eastward over the single-track Trans-Siberian Railway that still had a gap at Lake Baikal, arrived in Manchuria in pieces and was outmaneuvered at every encounter. The Japanese took the heights above Port Arthur in December after some of the bloodiest infantry assaults of the new century, and the fortress fell on January 2, 1905. At Mukden, in late February, half a million men fought for two weeks in snow and mud; the Russians lost ninety thousand and abandoned the field.

The Baltic Fleet was the last card. Admiral Rozhestvensky took it out of Libau in October 1904 and sailed it eighteen thousand miles around Africa, his crews bickering, his coal supply uncertain, his ships shedding boilers and morale as they crawled south. In the North Sea, near the Dogger Bank, jumpy Russian gunners opened fire on British fishing trawlers in the belief that they were Japanese torpedo boats. Britain nearly went to war. The fleet sailed on. In May 1905, in the Tsushima Strait between Korea and Japan, Admiral Togo's faster, better-gunned ships caught it crossing in column and destroyed it in a single afternoon. Of thirty-eight Russian vessels, all but a handful were sunk, captured, or interned. The naval power of a European empire had been wiped out by an Asian one.

Theodore Roosevelt brokered a settlement at Portsmouth, New Hampshire, in the summer of 1905; Sergei Witte represented Russia and managed, by sheer presence and stubbornness, to limit the damage to the southern half of Sakhalin and the abandonment of Russian positions in Manchuria and Korea. It was a diplomat's triumph wrapped around a military catastrophe. Witte came home with the title of count and the contempt of the court for having signed anything at all.

For the regime, the meaning of the war was simple and cruel. The tsar's army could not protect the empire. The tsar's navy was at the bottom of the sea. The reserves called up from peasant villages had marched off without enthusiasm and come home, those who came home, with stories. The little father in Petersburg, it turned out, was not invincible. He might not even be competent.

By the time anyone in the Winter Palace understood this, the city was already moving.

Bloody Sunday

The priest was small, dark, charismatic, and almost certainly working for the police, although the exact terms of the arrangement have never been settled. Father Georgi Gapon ran an organization called the Assembly of Russian Factory and Mill Workers of the City of St. Petersburg, founded with the blessing of the Okhrana on the theory that workers given a tame, religious, patriotic outlet for their grievances would be less likely to listen to socialists. The theory worked rather too well. By the winter of 1904, Gapon's Assembly had eight thousand members and a momentum its sponsors had not anticipated.

In early January 1905, four workers at the Putilov ironworks were dismissed. The Assembly called a strike in their support. Within days, more than a hundred thousand men were off the job across the capital. Bakeries closed. Lights went out in apartment blocks where electricity depended on factory generators. Gapon, riding the crest of something he no longer controlled, conceived the idea of marching to the Winter Palace and presenting a petition directly to the tsar.

The petition itself was a remarkable document, half supplication and half manifesto. It addressed Nicholas as "Sire" and described the petitioners as his children. It asked for an eight-hour day, a minimum wage, the right to form unions, freedom of speech and religion, an end to the war, and a constituent assembly elected by universal suffrage. "We have no strength, O Sovereign," it read at one point. "Our patience is at an end. The terrible moment has come for us when death is better than the prolongation of our intolerable sufferings."

Sunday, January 22, 1905 - January 9 by the old Russian calendar - was clear and very cold. Several columns of marchers, perhaps two hundred thousand people in all, set out from the workers' districts toward the city center. They carried icons, crosses, and portraits of the tsar. Many had brought their wives and children. They sang hymns. Gapon, in his cassock, walked at the head of one of the columns. Nicholas was not in the city; he was at Tsarskoe Selo, and had been told nothing useful about what was coming.

The troops who blocked the bridges and the approaches to Palace Square were nervous garrison units, many of them reinforced overnight from outside the city. There was no central decision to fire; there were a dozen local decisions. At the Narva Gate, cavalry charged and then infantry volleyed into the head of Gapon's column. At the Troitsky Bridge, at the Shlisselburg gate, in front of the Alexander Garden, the same scene repeated. Men crumpled in the snow. Women screamed and ran. Children were trampled. The official count was around 130 dead and several hundred wounded; the count whispered through the city the next day was several times that.

Gapon survived, shaved his beard, escaped abroad, and within a year was hanged by his former comrades as a police agent. The petitioners survived, most of them, and went home. What did not survive was the idea that bound the whole edifice together: the idea that the tsar was the father of his people, separated from them only by wicked bureaucrats, and that if the people could only reach him he would understand. After January 22 there were many ways to feel about Nicholas II, but innocence was no longer one of them.

Within weeks the strikes had spread from Petersburg to Moscow, Warsaw, Riga, Baku, Odessa. Peasants began burning manor houses in the black-earth provinces. By summer, sailors on the battleship *Potemkin* in the Black Sea had mutinied, shot their officers, and steamed into Odessa harbor flying the red flag. The empire was coming apart.

The October Manifesto and the Duma

Through the spring and summer the regime tried half-measures. A commission was appointed to study workers' grievances. An edict on religious toleration was issued. In August, with the war already lost in fact if not yet on paper, Nicholas announced the creation of a consultative assembly - a Duma - chosen by a narrow franchise and empowered only to advise. This was the so-called Bulygin Duma, named after the interior minister who drafted it, and nobody outside the palace took it seriously. The liberals refused to participate. The socialists laughed.

What broke the regime was the general strike of October. It began with the railwaymen and spread within a week to almost every industry in European Russia. Trains stopped. Telegraph lines fell silent. Newspapers ceased to appear, then reappeared in unauthorized editions printing whatever they liked. Shops closed; theaters went dark; even some of the imperial ballet went on strike. In St. Petersburg, delegates from the striking factories formed a Council - in Russian, a Soviet - that for fifty days functioned as a kind of shadow city government. Its chairman, for most of that period, was a young lawyer named Leon Trotsky, recently returned from exile.

At Peterhof, Nicholas was presented with two options. The first, urged by his uncle Grand Duke Nicholas Nikolaevich, was a military dictatorship; the Grand Duke is supposed to have drawn a revolver in the tsar's study and threatened to shoot himself if his nephew refused to compromise. The second, urged by Witte, was to grant a constitution. Nicholas signed the manifesto that Witte put before him on October 30 with what he later called the most painful day of his life. "There was no other way out," he wrote to his mother, "than to cross oneself and grant what everyone was asking for."

The October Manifesto promised freedom of conscience, speech, assembly, and association. It promised that no law would take effect without the approval of an elected Duma. It promised that the suffrage would be broadened. In the language of European constitutionalism, it converted Russia overnight from an autocracy into something else - what, exactly, no one was sure.

The reaction in the streets was euphoric, then divided, then ugly. Liberals - lawyers, professors, zemstvo activists - founded a party, the Constitutional Democrats or Kadets, and prepared to make the new system work. Socialists denounced the manifesto as a trick and called for the strike to continue; the Petersburg Soviet held out until early December, when its leaders were arrested. In the Pale of Settlement and in dozens of provincial towns, far-right mobs, often with police complicity, attacked Jews in pogroms whose savagery shocked even contemporaries hardened to such things. In Moscow in December, a workers' uprising in the Presnya district was crushed by artillery; whole streets were leveled, hundreds killed.

The first Duma met in the Tauride Palace in April 1906. It was a remarkable body - peasants in homespun, professors in frock coats, Polish nationalists, Muslim deputies from the Caucasus and Central Asia, lawyers who had spent careers defending political prisoners. It was also, from the regime's point of view, impossible. It demanded amnesty for political offenders, abolition of the State Council that had been hastily inserted as an upper chamber, redistribution of land. The government refused. After seventy-two days, Nicholas dissolved it. A second Duma, elected on the same franchise, proved no more pliable, and was dissolved in June 1907. New electoral laws then sharply restricted the franchise, weighting it toward landowners and the wealthy. The third and fourth Dumas, elected under these rules, were tame.

What Russia had, by the end of 1907, was a semi-constitutional regime in which the constitution was honored selectively, the parliament met but did not legislate freely, and the autocracy continued to call itself an autocracy. The settlement satisfied no one. It would have to be defended by someone harder than Witte.

Stolypin's Wager

Pyotr Stolypin came to office in the summer of 1906, at the age of forty-four, with the reputation of a provincial governor who had hanged revolutionaries in Saratov without losing sleep. He was tall, square-shouldered, bearded, and entirely without the diffidence of his sovereign. Within weeks of his appointment as prime minister, terrorists threw a bomb into his villa on Aptekarsky Island, killing twenty-seven people and wounding his daughter and son. Stolypin himself was unhurt. He went back to work the next day.

His program had two halves, and he meant them to work together. The first half was repression. Military field courts, established by emergency decree, tried suspected terrorists within twenty-four hours and hanged them within twenty-four more. Over a thousand people were executed in 1906 and 1907; the noose became known as Stolypin's necktie, the prison transport car as Stolypin's carriage. The Socialist Revolutionary Combat Organization, which had killed two interior ministers and a grand duke, was hunted into near-extinction. Strikes were broken. Newspapers were closed.

The second half was the wager. Stolypin had concluded, watching the peasant disorders of 1905 and 1906, that the village commune - the *obshchina*, with its periodic redistribution of strips of land - was the breeding ground of rural radicalism. A peasant who held his land in common with his neighbors, and whose share might be reshuffled every few years, had no incentive to improve it and every incentive to envy his betters. A peasant who owned his land outright, consolidated into a single farm, would be a conservative. He would have something to lose. He would be, in Stolypin's phrase, a wager not on the drunk and the weak, but on the sober and the strong.

The decrees of November 1906 allowed any peasant household to withdraw from the commune and claim its share of land as private property. Subsequent legislation provided for the consolidation of scattered strips into single holdings and offered cheap credit through a Peasant Land Bank. A parallel program subsidized migration to Siberia, where some three million peasants moved between 1906 and 1914, breaking ground that had never been plowed.

The reform worked, in part. By 1914 something like a quarter of peasant households had left the commune. Grain exports rose. A class of relatively prosperous farmers, the so-called *kulaks*, began to thicken in the more fertile provinces. Cooperative societies multiplied. Stolypin had asked for twenty years of peace, foreign and domestic, in which to complete the work, and he predicted that at the end of that time Russia would be unrecognizable.

He did not get twenty years. He did not get five. In September 1911, at a gala performance of Rimsky-Korsakov's *The Tale of Tsar Saltan* at the Kiev Opera House, a young man named Dmitri Bogrov walked up to Stolypin during the second intermission and shot him twice in the chest. Bogrov was a revolutionary; he was also a police informer; the exact arrangement, as with Gapon six years earlier, was never satisfactorily explained. Stolypin died four days later. Nicholas attended the funeral and within months had begun to speak of him with the cool dismissiveness he reserved for ministers who had pressed him too hard.

In the front pew at the Kiev cathedral that day sat a tsar who had now outlived two prime ministers who had tried to save him. The country outside the cathedral was quieter than it had been in 1905, the strikes fewer, the harvests better, the executions still proceeding in the provincial courtyards. The factories of Petersburg were running three shifts. In the workshops, men who had marched with Gapon were teaching their younger brothers what they had learned about the troops on the bridges.

The factories of Petersburg ran three shifts and the men who had marched with Gapon taught their younger brothers about the troops on the bridges. The lessons of 1905 had been absorbed by both sides, and both sides believed they had learned the right ones. The tsar believed he had survived. The workers believed they had glimpsed something that could be reached again. What neither side had factored in was the war that would arrive in 1914 and grind the country between them, until the bread queues began forming before dawn and the patience that had held since 1905 finally gave out.

Chapter 12
The Year of Two Revolutions

Russia at War

By the winter of 1916, the bread queues in Petrograd began forming before dawn. Women stood in the cold for hours, sometimes for nothing. The bakeries opened, sold what they had, and closed. Flour was somewhere - in railway sidings, in warehouses, in fields that had never been harvested because the men who should have harvested them were dead or at the front or sitting in trenches waiting to be one or the other.

The war had eaten Russia from the inside. When it began in 1914, crowds had cheered the Tsar on the balcony of the Winter Palace. The capital had been renamed Petrograd because St. Petersburg sounded too German. The Duma had voted credits. Priests had blessed regiments. Within two years almost none of that goodwill remained.

The army had taken in millions of peasants and given many of them rifles, sometimes one between two men. Casualties ran into the millions. Whole formations dissolved in retreat through Galicia and Poland in 1915. Officers shot deserters and were shot in turn by their own men. Soldiers wrote home, and what they wrote, when it got through, was that the war was lost and that the generals were fools and that the Tsar's wife was a German.

That last accusation mattered more than it should have. Empress Alexandra was a granddaughter of Queen Victoria, raised in Hesse, devoted to Orthodoxy with the intensity of a convert and to her hemophiliac son with the ferocity of any mother watching a child bleed. She had also fallen under the influence of Grigori Rasputin, a Siberian holy man whose presence at court was a gift to every gossip in the empire. When Nicholas II left for army headquarters at Mogilev in 1915 to take personal command of the war, he left the capital to his wife and, by extension, to Rasputin. Ministers came and went. The Duma met, was suspended, met again. In December 1916 a group of aristocrats murdered Rasputin in a cellar on the Moika Canal, shooting him and dumping him through the ice. The killing solved nothing. What lay beneath Rasputin was a state that no longer worked.

The railways were the clearest measure of the collapse. Russia had built them to carry grain west and soldiers anywhere. By 1917 locomotives were breaking down faster than they could be repaired. Coal sat at the pithead. Grain sat in the Volga provinces. In Petrograd, a city of two and a half million, the food simply did not arrive in the quantities needed, and what arrived cost more than a factory worker earned. Wages had doubled since 1914; the price of bread had risen far more.

The factories of the capital had swollen with the war. Putilov, the great metalworks on the southwestern edge of the city, employed tens of thousands. Men and women worked twelve-hour shifts producing shells, then went home to apartments where the stove had no fuel. Strikes were illegal. Strikes happened anyway. The Okhrana, the secret police, reported in January 1917 that the mood in the working districts was worse than at any time since 1905, and that something would break soon.

Nicholas read these reports at Mogilev, where he played dominoes with his staff and walked his daughters' spaniel along the Dnieper. He believed the army was still loyal. He believed the people loved their Tsar. He believed the war could be won in a final spring offensive. He was wrong about all three, and the proof began on a Thursday in late February when the women of the Vyborg district walked off their shifts to mark International Women's Day and to demand bread.

February: The Tsar Abdicates

It started as a march and turned into something else by lunchtime. The women from the textile mills crossed the Liteiny Bridge and pulled men out of the metalworks. By evening tens of thousands were on the streets of central Petrograd. The next day there were more. By Saturday the central districts were impassable and the crowds were shouting not just for bread but for an end to the war and an end to the autocracy.

The garrison of Petrograd was the key. There were nearly two hundred thousand soldiers in the capital, most of them reserves who had been told they would soon be sent to the front. They were peasants in uniform, badly trained, badly housed, and not eager to die in Galicia. On Sunday, February 26, troops fired on demonstrators in several places, killing dozens. That night the soldiers of the Volynsky Regiment talked over what they had done and decided not to do it again.

On Monday morning they shot their commanding officer instead. Then they marched out of their barracks and began calling on the other regiments to join them. By the end of the day most of the garrison had gone over. Crowds opened the prisons, burned police stations, hunted down officers in the street. The arsenal at the Peter and Paul Fortress was thrown open. Workers and soldiers seized the Tauride Palace, where the Duma met, and demanded that the deputies do something.

The deputies hesitated. They were monarchists and liberals and moderate socialists, and none of them had planned a revolution. They were also being shouted at by armed men in greatcoats. They formed a committee. Down the corridor, in another hall of the same palace, workers' and soldiers' representatives formed a different committee and called it the Petrograd Soviet, reviving the name from 1905. The Duma committee would soon call itself the Provisional Government. The two bodies sat in the same building and looked at each other warily.

Nicholas, at Mogilev, ordered loyal troops sent to put the rising down. The orders were obeyed and then countermanded and then ignored. The general he sent ahead, Ivanov, found that the railway workers would not move his train where he wanted it to go. Nicholas himself boarded the imperial train to return to Petrograd and got as far as Pskov, where his generals stopped him and told him the truth.

They told him the garrison was lost, the capital was lost, the front-line commanders had been polled, and every one of them advised abdication. He took the news the way he took most news, with a calm that read either as faith or as inability to feel what was happening. He went to his private carriage and wrote in his diary that there was treason and cowardice and deceit on every side.

On the evening of March 2, in the dining car of the train at Pskov station, he signed the document. He abdicated for himself and, in a clause his advisors had not expected, for his son as well; the boy was ill and the father would not be separated from him. The crown passed to his brother, Grand Duke Mikhail. The next day Mikhail, after meeting with the new government and being told no one could guarantee his safety, declined it.

Three hundred and four years of Romanov rule ended in two signatures and a railway carriage. There was no battle. There was no last stand. The dynasty that had outlasted Napoleon and broken the Decembrists and survived 1905 simply stopped, because the man at the top of it had no idea what to do, and the men around him no longer believed there was anything to do but end it. In Petrograd that night the red flags went up on the spire of the Admiralty. The new government sent a telegram to its allies in London and Paris promising to fight on.

Dual Power and Lenin's Return

The promise to fight on was the first mistake, and it was made because there was no real alternative the new government could imagine. The men who took office in March - liberal lawyers, professors, landowners with progressive views - had spent their political lives in opposition to autocracy, not in opposition to the war. They believed Russia's honor depended on seeing it through. They also believed that the Petrograd Soviet, which they did not control, would let them.

This was the arrangement that became known as dual power. The Provisional Government held the ministries and signed the decrees. The Soviet held the loyalty of the soldiers and the workers. The first significant act of the Soviet, Order Number One, instructed soldiers to form committees in every unit and to obey the Provisional Government only insofar as its orders did not contradict the Soviet's. The army's chain of command, already fraying, came apart in weeks.

Alexander Kerensky was the bridge between the two bodies. A lawyer in his thirties, a Socialist Revolutionary, theatrical, energetic, the only man who held a seat in both, he became Minister of Justice, then Minister of War, then in July prime minister. He gave speeches that made audiences weep. He toured the front in an open car. He believed in the revolution and in the war and in himself, in that order or perhaps the reverse.

Into this arrangement, on the evening of April 3, stepped a small bald man in a bowler hat at the Finland Station. Vladimir Lenin had spent the war in Switzerland, writing pamphlets that almost no one read, watching the European socialist parties he had counted on vote credits for their own armies. When news of the February Revolution reached Zurich he was desperate to get home. The Germans, who had every reason to want Russia in chaos, agreed to move him across their territory in a sealed train. They paid for the ticket and would later pay for much else.

He arrived in Petrograd expecting to find his own party, the Bolsheviks, embracing the revolution like everyone else. He found Stalin and Kamenev offering critical support to the Provisional Government. He climbed onto an armored car outside the station and told the crowd, and his own comrades, that they were wrong. There would be no support for this government. There would be no defense of this war. All power to the Soviets. Bread, peace, land.

The April Theses, as the program became known, struck most observers as the ravings of a man who had been away too long. Even within the Bolshevik leadership the reception was cold. Lenin argued, browbeat, threatened to resign, and within a few weeks brought the party around. The slogans were simple, repeatable, and answered the three questions every Russian was asking: when would the war end, when would the peasants get the land, when would there be food.

The Provisional Government answered none of them. It postponed the land question until a Constituent Assembly could be elected, then postponed the assembly. It launched a major offensive in June, the brainchild of Kerensky and the new commander Brusilov, designed to prove that revolutionary Russia could still fight. The offensive collapsed within days. Soldiers refused to advance. Entire regiments walked away from the front and started home, often by stealing trains.

In July, a half-spontaneous rising in Petrograd by sailors and workers turned into a Bolshevik moment that the Bolsheviks were not ready for. The government released documents suggesting Lenin was a German agent. The party was driven underground. Lenin fled to Finland, shaved his beard, hid in a haystack outside the capital. Trotsky, who had joined the Bolsheviks only weeks earlier, was arrested. It looked, in that summer, like the party might be finished.

What saved it was a general. In late August, Lavr Kornilov, the new commander-in-chief, a Cossack with a reputation for iron, marched troops toward Petrograd. Whether he intended to crush the Soviet only, or the Provisional Government as well, was unclear at the time and remains so. Kerensky panicked, called him a traitor, and asked the Soviet for help. The Soviet asked the Bolsheviks. The Bolsheviks emerged from underground to arm the workers of Petrograd. Kornilov's troops never reached the city; railway workers blocked their trains and agitators talked the soldiers out of fighting. The guns the Bolsheviks were given that week were not given back.

October: The Bolsheviks Take Power

By October, Lenin was back in the capital in disguise, demanding that the party seize power before the Constituent Assembly could meet and before the Germans could take Petrograd. He wrote letters in a fury, threatening to resign if the Central Committee did not act. On October 10, in an apartment on the Karpovka Embankment, the committee voted by ten to two for armed insurrection. The two against were Kamenev and Zinoviev. A week later they leaked the decision to a non-party newspaper. Lenin called for their expulsion. The insurrection went ahead anyway.

The instrument was the Military Revolutionary Committee of the Petrograd Soviet, chaired by Trotsky. On paper it existed to defend the city against the Germans and against any second Kornilov. In practice it issued orders to the garrison, and the garrison, by now thoroughly Bolshevized, obeyed them rather than the Provisional Government. Trotsky understood that this gave the party everything it needed. The seizure of power could be dressed not as a coup but as the Soviet defending itself.

The trigger came on October 24. Kerensky, finally moving, ordered the closure of two Bolshevik newspapers and called loyal troops into the city. There were not many loyal troops. The Military Revolutionary Committee responded by sending Red Guards and soldiers to occupy the telephone exchange, the telegraph, the railway stations, the bridges, the state bank. They did this through the night and into the next day, mostly without firing a shot. Trams ran. Theaters opened. Most of the city had no idea that a revolution was happening around it.

By the afternoon of October 25, the Provisional Government held only the Winter Palace, defended by a few hundred cadets, a company of Cossacks, and the Women's Battalion of Death. Kerensky himself had already left the city in a car borrowed from the American embassy, looking for troops at the front who might still rally to him. He would not find them.

The taking of the Winter Palace, later painted as the storming of a fortress, was something smaller and stranger. The cruiser Aurora, moored on the Neva, fired a blank round around nine in the evening. There was desultory shooting around the palace through the night. Red Guards and soldiers drifted in through unguarded side entrances, got lost in the corridors, looted the wine cellars. By two in the morning, a small detachment found the cabinet of the Provisional Government in the Malachite Room and arrested them. The casualties of the night ran into the single digits.

While this was happening, the Second Congress of Soviets was meeting at the Smolny Institute, a former girls' school across the city. The hall was full of soldiers and workers' delegates, the air thick with cigarette smoke. The Mensheviks and right Socialist Revolutionaries denounced the insurrection as adventurism and walked out. Trotsky, from the platform, told them they were going where they belonged - to the dustbin of history.

The remaining delegates ratified the seizure of power. Lenin, emerging from hiding, took the platform to applause that went on for minutes. He announced that they would now proceed to construct the socialist order. Two decrees were passed that night. The Decree on Peace offered immediate negotiations for an end to the war without annexations or indemnities. The Decree on Land abolished private ownership of land and transferred it to peasant committees - a policy lifted almost verbatim from the Socialist Revolutionary program, because Lenin knew the peasants would not fight for anyone else's.

A new government was formed, called the Council of People's Commissars, with Lenin at its head. Trotsky took foreign affairs. Stalin took nationalities. Almost no one outside Petrograd had heard most of the names, and almost no one believed the new government would last more than a few weeks. Foreign ambassadors sent home dispatches predicting collapse by Christmas. The Constituent Assembly, when it finally met in January 1918, was dissolved by armed sailors after a single day because the Bolsheviks had not won a majority. The party that nobody had taken seriously in the summer now ran the capital, the army, the banks, and the printing presses. What it did not yet run was the country.

Brest-Litovsk and the Cost of Peace

Peace was the promise the Bolsheviks had ridden to power, and it was the promise they were least able to keep on their own terms. The Decree on Peace called on all warring nations to negotiate. Only Germany answered. Britain and France had no interest in a treaty that would let the Germans move every division on the Eastern Front to the west.

Talks opened in December 1917 at Brest-Litovsk, a town in the marshes that the Germans had taken in 1915. Trotsky led the Russian delegation. The German terms, when they came, were monstrous: Poland, Lithuania, Courland, much of Belarus and Ukraine to be detached from Russia, to become German client states or to be annexed outright. A third of the empire's population, half its industry, most of its coal.

Inside the Bolshevik leadership the argument was savage. Lenin wanted to sign. He argued that the revolution needed any peace it could get, that the army no longer existed in any meaningful sense, that the regime would not survive another campaign. Bukharin and the Left Communists wanted a revolutionary war, a guerrilla rising of armed workers against German imperialism, on the assumption that the German workers would soon rise too. Trotsky proposed something in between, a formula he called "neither war nor peace": declare hostilities ended, refuse to sign, walk out, and see what the Germans dared to do.

What the Germans dared to do was resume their advance in February 1918. They met no resistance. They took Kiev, Minsk, Pskov, threatened Petrograd itself. Lenin, in the Central Committee, threatened resignation, won the vote by a narrow margin, and accepted terms worse than the original ones. The Treaty of Brest-Litovsk was signed on March 3, 1918. The government had already moved the capital to Moscow, where the Kremlin walls offered some sense of distance from the German army.

The territorial losses on paper were enormous. Finland, the Baltic provinces, Poland, Ukraine - all gone. Bessarabia gone to Romania. The Caucasus uncertain. In exchange the Bolsheviks bought time, which was the only thing they actually had to spend.

The cost did not stop at the borders. The treaty broke what remained of the alliance with the Left Socialist Revolutionaries, who had been junior partners in the government and who now resigned in protest. It gave the Allies a reason to land troops at Murmansk, Arkhangelsk, Vladivostok. It hardened every officer who had been wavering into a determination to fight the Bolsheviks. The Czechoslovak Legion, forty thousand armed men strung out along the Trans-Siberian Railway, mutinied that May. White armies began to form in the south, the east, the north. By summer the country was at war with itself.

In November the German revolution Bukharin had predicted actually happened. The Kaiser abdicated. The Western Front collapsed. The treaty Lenin had signed in March became, overnight, a worthless piece of paper, and the Soviet government formally annulled it. But the territories were not recovered by signature. They would have to be fought for, and the army that would do the fighting was only beginning to be built, in a country where the trains had stopped running, the cities were starving, and the men with guns no longer agreed on who they were fighting for.

On a wall in Moscow that winter someone had chalked the new slogan in uneven letters: All Power to the Soviets. Below it, in a different hand, someone had written: And what shall we eat.

All Power to the Soviets, the wall said, and underneath, in the other hand, the harder question. The Bolsheviks had taken the capital with surprising ease. Holding the country was a different matter. The territories signed away at Brest-Litovsk would have to be fought for, and so would the cities, and the railways, and the grain. The army that would do the fighting did not yet exist. The man who would build it was on a train, dictating orders in a railway carriage, and the war that followed would kill more Russians than the Great War had.

Chapter 13
Civil War and the Birth of the Soviet State

The Whites, the Reds, and the Greens

In the winter of 1918, a young officer named Trotsky stood in a railway carriage outside Moscow and dictated orders that would, over the next three years, kill more Russians than the Great War had. He had no military background. He had spent most of the previous decade in exile, arguing about Marx in cafés. Now he commanded an army that did not yet exist, against enemies converging on the new Bolshevik government from every direction at once.

The Bolsheviks had taken Petrograd in November 1917 with surprising ease. Holding Russia was another matter. By the spring of 1918 the country had begun to splinter into a war that no one quite controlled and no one could quite name. It was called, when it was given a name at all, the Civil War - but it was actually several wars running in parallel: a war between Reds and Whites, a war between peasants and the state, a war among nationalities, and a war in which British, French, American, Japanese, and Czechoslovak troops all found themselves, for their own reasons, fighting on Russian soil.

The Whites were never a single thing. They were tsarist generals like Denikin and Kolchak, Cossack hosts on the Don, liberal politicians thrown out of the Constituent Assembly, and socialists who hated the Bolsheviks more than they hated the old regime. What they shared was opposition to Lenin and a chronic inability to agree on anything else. A monarchist colonel in Siberia and a republican lawyer in the south might find themselves nominally on the same side, but they could not write a common program, could not coordinate offensives, and could not decide what Russia would be if they won. They had foreign money, foreign weapons, and at various moments foreign soldiers. They did not have a plausible future to offer a peasant.

The Reds had the center. They held Moscow and Petrograd, the arms factories, most of the railway hubs, and the bulk of the European Russian population. Trotsky took an army of volunteers and deserters and former tsarist officers - he conscripted those officers, held their families hostage, and shot the ones who failed - and turned it into a force of millions. He traveled in his armored train from front to front, arriving at points of collapse with revolvers, medals, leather coats, and execution squads. The Red Army was crueler to its own than the Whites were to theirs, and it worked.

Then there were the Greens. Historians use the word loosely. It covered peasant bands who fought whoever came to take their grain or their sons; it covered Nestor Makhno's anarchist army in Ukraine, which at its peak controlled a territory the size of a small European country and fought Whites, Reds, Germans, and Ukrainian nationalists in turn; it covered the deserters in the forests who simply wanted to be left alone. The Greens almost never won, but they made the countryside impossible to govern. A Red regiment could march through a village in the morning, a White detachment could arrive in the afternoon, and a Green band could burn the grain store at night. In some districts power changed hands a dozen times in a year.

By 1920 the main White armies had been broken. Kolchak was shot in Irkutsk. Denikin was driven out of the south; his successor Wrangel was evacuated from Crimea by the French fleet, carrying the last remnants of the old officer class into a permanent exile that would scatter them through Paris, Belgrade, Harbin, and Buenos Aires. The Reds had won the conventional war. The other wars - against the peasants, against famine, against their own promises - were only beginning.

War Communism and the Cheka

The system the Bolsheviks built to fight the Civil War was called War Communism, although the name came later and the policy was less a plan than a series of emergencies treated as principles. Factories were nationalized. Money lost most of its meaning as inflation destroyed the ruble. Workers were paid in bread rations and boots. Trade was outlawed and then carried on anyway, illegally, by women with sacks on their backs who walked out of the cities into the villages to exchange a wedding ring for a few pounds of flour. The Bolsheviks called them speculators and sometimes shot them.

The center of the system was grain requisitioning. Armed detachments went into the villages and took what they decided the village did not need. They were supposed to take surpluses. They took what they could find. They dug up cellars, broke open floors, beat headmen, and shot those they identified as kulaks - a word that was supposed to mean prosperous peasant but in practice meant any peasant who resisted. The grain fed the Red Army and the cities. What was left did not always feed the village. The peasants responded as peasants have always responded to such things: they hid grain, planted less, and killed their livestock rather than have it taken. By 1920 the sown area in European Russia had fallen by something like a third, and in some provinces by far more. The country that fed Europe before the war could no longer feed itself.

To enforce all of this there was the Cheka. It had been founded in December 1917, a few weeks after the seizure of power, under a Polish nobleman turned revolutionary named Felix Dzerzhinsky. He was ascetic, sleepless, incorruptible, and entirely without scruple about means. The Cheka began as a small body for fighting sabotage and counter-revolution. It grew, in the course of the Civil War, into something for which the Russian language did not yet have a word and which the twentieth century would learn to recognize: a political police with its own prisons, its own troops, its own courts, and the authority to shoot on its own warrant.

The Red Terror was declared formally in September 1918, after an attempt on Lenin's life left him wounded and the head of the Petrograd Cheka was assassinated the same week. Hostages were taken from the old propertied classes and shot in batches. Estimates of the dead during the Civil War years range widely; the most careful historians suggest the Cheka killed somewhere between fifty thousand and two hundred thousand people directly, with many more dying in its camps and prisons. The numbers are imprecise because the Cheka kept records that were both meticulous and incomplete, and because in many provinces local commanders simply killed people and did not write it down.

Dzerzhinsky defended all of it without embarrassment. The Cheka, he said, stood for organized terror. It was not a court and it was not interested in evidence. It existed to identify enemies of the revolution and remove them. He meant the words exactly as they sounded.

What is harder to capture, at this distance, is how many of the men and women who staffed this apparatus believed in it. They were not, most of them, cynics. They were former workers, former students, former soldiers who had decided that the revolution was the one thing in the world worth doing and that anything protecting it was therefore justified. They wrote earnest letters home about the necessity of severity. They went hungry alongside the people they policed. Some shot themselves when they could no longer bear what they had done. Most kept working. By 1921 the apparatus was permanent. The Civil War would end. The Cheka, under various initials - GPU, OGPU, NKVD, KGB - would not.

The Killing of the Romanovs

The Romanovs spent the spring of 1918 in a merchant's house in Yekaterinburg, in the Urals, behind whitewashed windows and a high wooden fence. Nicholas read aloud to his children in the evenings. Alexandra wrote in her diary about the weather and her son's health. The four daughters sewed jewels into the linings of their dresses, in case they were ever moved again. They were guarded by a rotating detachment of local Bolsheviks who at first stole their things and were rude to them, and then, as the months passed, became something closer to companions - and were eventually replaced because the local soviet did not trust them anymore.

By July the Czechoslovak Legion was advancing on Yekaterinburg from the east. The town would fall within days. Moscow did not want the tsar to be rescued and become a banner. What was decided, and by whom, has been argued about ever since. Lenin's direct order has never been found in writing. The local Ural soviet acted, and Moscow did not stop them, and Lenin appears to have approved after the fact, if not before.

On the night of July 16, 1918, the family was woken and told to dress. They were taken down to a basement room and arranged as if for a photograph - Nicholas standing in front, Alexandra in a chair, the children behind, the doctor and three servants along the wall. The commandant, Yakov Yurovsky, read out a short sentence from the Ural Regional Soviet. Nicholas turned to his family and said something the surviving accounts disagree about. Then the squad began to fire.

It was botched. The jewels in the daughters' dresses deflected the first bullets. The room filled with smoke. The killers had to finish the work with bayonets and revolvers at close range. It took something like twenty minutes. The bodies were carried out in a truck, driven into the forest, stripped, mutilated with acid, and dumped down a mine shaft. The next day the bodies were moved again, hastily, to a pit a few miles away and covered over. They would lie there, undisturbed, for sixty years.

The Bolsheviks announced the death of Nicholas and said nothing for some time about the rest of the family. The fiction that Alexandra and the children might still be alive was useful for a while, and then it was not, and then it was quietly dropped. What had been killed in the basement was not only seven people and four servants - it was also the possibility of restoration. There was no longer a tsar to put back on a throne. The Whites who marched into Yekaterinburg a week later understood this, walked through the empty house, found bloodstains and a few buttons, and went on fighting for a cause that had just lost its center.

Famine and the New Economic Policy

The famine began in the Volga in 1921. It had been building for years - the war, the requisitioning, the collapse of transport, the drought of that summer - and when it arrived it killed on a scale the Russian state had not seen since the seventeenth century. Estimates vary; five million dead is a common figure, and some go considerably higher. Whole villages emptied. Refugees walked east, then west, then died in the railway stations. There were verified cases of cannibalism in the worst-hit districts. Photographs from the relief expeditions show children whose skin has gone tight over their skulls and whose eyes are too large for their faces.

The Soviet government, having spent four years denouncing foreign capital, asked for help. The American Relief Administration, run by Herbert Hoover, fed something like ten million people at the peak of the operation. Quakers worked alongside Bolsheviks. Trains carrying American corn moved across a country whose government had recently been at war with American expeditionary forces. The contradictions were noted by everyone and acted on by no one, because the alternative was watching more children die.

While the famine was killing the countryside, the cities were emptying. Petrograd had lost roughly two thirds of its population since 1917. Workers had gone back to the villages to look for food. The proletariat in whose name the Bolsheviks ruled had largely ceased to exist as an organized class. And in February 1921 the sailors of the Kronstadt naval base - men who had been among the most radical supporters of the revolution in 1917 - rose in mutiny against the government they had helped to put in power. They demanded free elections to the soviets, freedom of speech for socialists, an end to grain requisitioning. They were crushed by Trotsky's troops, who crossed the ice to take the fortress. Several thousand were killed in the assault. Many of the survivors were shot afterward.

Kronstadt frightened Lenin in a way the White armies had not. The Whites had been outsiders. Kronstadt was inside the family. Within weeks of the mutiny, at the Tenth Party Congress, Lenin announced what he called the New Economic Policy. Grain requisitioning would be replaced by a tax in kind. Peasants would be allowed to sell their surpluses. Small businesses could reopen. Foreign concessions would be permitted. Money would be reintroduced, and a new ruble would be issued and stabilized. The state kept what Lenin called the commanding heights - heavy industry, banking, foreign trade, the railways. Everything else could, for the moment, be left to the market.

Lenin defended the retreat to his party with characteristic directness. They had tried to leap directly to socialism, he said, and they had failed. They would now do something more modest. The effects were almost immediate. Markets reopened in the cities. Peasants who had spent four years hiding grain began to bring it out. The famine eased, then ended. By 1923 a class of small traders had reappeared - the so-called Nepmen, in fur coats and bowler hats, eating in restaurants that had been closed since the revolution. Old Bolsheviks looked at them and felt sick. They had not fought a civil war to see speculators in fur coats. But they were eating better than they had in years, and so were the workers, and so were the peasants, and the regime did not fall.

The NEP would last, in various forms, until the end of the decade. It was always understood by its supporters as a tactical retreat, and by its opponents within the party as a betrayal. Both descriptions had something to them. Lenin called it a temporary measure. He did not say how temporary.

Lenin's Last Years and Succession

In May 1922 Lenin suffered his first stroke. He was fifty-two. He recovered enough to work through the summer, then suffered a second stroke in December, and a third in March 1923 that left him unable to speak. He lived another ten months, mostly at the dacha at Gorki, attended by his wife Krupskaya and his sister Maria, watched by doctors and watched, more discreetly, by Stalin's secretariat. He died on January 21, 1924.

Between the strokes he had been trying to do something he had never had time for before: think about what would happen after him. The result was a series of dictated notes that came to be called his Testament. He went through the leading members of the Politburo one by one. Trotsky was the most able man in the Central Committee, but too self-confident and too taken with administrative matters. Zinoviev and Kamenev had failings he was prepared to overlook but his readers should remember. Bukharin was the favorite of the party but had never fully understood dialectics.

Then he came to Stalin. Stalin had concentrated enormous power in his hands as General Secretary, and Lenin was not sure he would always use it carefully enough. A few weeks later, after a quarrel in which Stalin had insulted Krupskaya on the telephone, Lenin added a postscript: Stalin was too rude. He should be removed from the post of General Secretary and replaced by someone more patient, more loyal, more attentive to comrades.

The Testament was read to a small group of senior party members after Lenin's death. They decided, with Stalin sitting in the room, not to publish it and not to act on it. Zinoviev and Kamenev led the argument for keeping Stalin in place. They were afraid of Trotsky, and they thought Stalin was a useful ally against him. Within four years both would be expelled from the party. Within fifteen, both would be shot.

Lenin's funeral was the largest the country had ever seen. The body was carried through Moscow in a freezing January cold so severe that the bearers' hands stuck to the coffin. Against the wishes of Krupskaya, who wanted a simple burial, the Politburo decided to embalm him. A mausoleum was thrown up in wood on Red Square, later replaced in granite. Lines began to form to see him and never really stopped.

The cult began at once. Cities were renamed - Petrograd became Leningrad. Statues went up. Quotations from Lenin became the way arguments were settled inside the party, which meant that whoever could most plausibly claim to speak for the dead man would inherit the living state. Stalin had been organizing the funeral. He had also been organizing the party apparatus for years, appointing secretaries in the provinces, building card files, accumulating the kind of bureaucratic power that no one else in the leadership had bothered to acquire because it seemed unglamorous.

Trotsky was not at the funeral. He had been ill, and Stalin, according to Trotsky's later account, had given him the wrong date for the ceremony. Whether or not this was true, it was widely believed, and it captured something real. Trotsky, the orator, the founder of the Red Army, the second man of the revolution, had been outmaneuvered in a way he did not yet understand by a man he had once dismissed as a gray blur, a mediocrity, the most eminent nonentity in the party.

In the spring after Lenin's death the snow melted on Red Square and the lines re-formed outside the wooden mausoleum. Inside, under glass, the small bald figure lay with his hands folded. Outside, the men who had won the Civil War were beginning to look at one another and calculate.

The lines re-formed outside the wooden mausoleum and the men who had won the civil war began to look at one another and calculate. The party Lenin had built was suddenly a party without a center. The obvious successor was the orator with the Red Army behind him. The actual successor was the man Trotsky had once dismissed as a gray blur, a mediocrity, the most eminent nonentity in the party. How that mistake was made, and what it cost, would shape the next quarter century of Russian life and the deaths of millions whose names were not yet on any list.

Chapter 14
Stalin: Revolution from Above

Outmaneuvering the Old Bolsheviks

In May 1922, Lenin suffered the first of the strokes that would kill him. He was fifty-two. The party he had built was suddenly a party without a center, and the men who had stood beside him in 1917 began, slowly and then quickly, to circle one another.

Joseph Dzhugashvili, the cobbler's son from Gori who had taken the name Stalin, was not the obvious heir. Trotsky was the orator, the organizer of the Red Army, the second name on every poster from the civil war years. Zinoviev ran Petrograd. Kamenev ran Moscow. Bukharin was the party's intellectual conscience, the man Lenin had called the favorite of the whole party. Stalin was the General Secretary, a post created in 1922 and widely treated as a clerical job - keeping files, assigning cadres, taking the minutes nobody wanted to take.

That was the mistake. The General Secretary controlled appointments, and appointments, in a one-party state, were everything. Every provincial committee, every factory cell, every regional soviet eventually owed its chairmanship to someone in Stalin's secretariat. By the time Lenin dictated his Testament in late 1922 - the document that warned the party Stalin had "concentrated enormous power in his hands" and recommended his removal - the network was already too dense to unwind. When Lenin died in January 1924, the Testament was read in closed session and quietly shelved. Stalin had the votes.

He moved against his rivals one at a time, and never against more than one faction at once. First he allied with Zinoviev and Kamenev against Trotsky, casting Trotsky as the dangerous left adventurer who wanted permanent revolution abroad while Russia starved at home. Stalin offered instead "socialism in one country" - a doctrine that sounded modest and was, in 1925, what an exhausted population wanted to hear. Trotsky was stripped of the War Commissariat in January 1925, ejected from the Politburo in 1926, expelled from the party in 1927, deported to Kazakhstan in 1928, and shipped out of the Soviet Union altogether in 1929.

Then Stalin turned on Zinoviev and Kamenev, who, having watched their ally devoured, belatedly tried to form a United Opposition. They were crushed in 1926 and 1927 by the same methods - control of the apparatus, control of the press, control of who got a hall to speak in and who did not. That left Bukharin and the right, the men who defended the New Economic Policy and the cautious accommodation with the peasantry. For two years Stalin had stood with them. In 1928, with no one left on his left flank, he turned. Bukharin was denounced for "right deviation," removed from the Politburo in 1929, and reduced to writing technical articles. He was shot in 1938 after confessing, in open court, to crimes he had not committed.

By the end of 1929 - Stalin's fiftieth birthday, marked by an avalanche of newspaper tributes that filled column after column with adjectives - he stood alone at the top of the party. The old Bolsheviks were not yet dead. Most still held offices, sat on committees, drew rations from the Kremlin canteen. But they served at his pleasure now, and they knew it.

What followed was something the party had never authorized and most of its founders would not have recognized. Stalin called it a revolution from above. It was directed not against the old ruling class, long since killed or exiled, but against the country itself.

Collectivization and the Ukrainian Famine

The grain crisis came first. In the winter of 1927-28, peasants held back their harvest from the state, refusing to sell at the artificially low prices Moscow offered. The cities began to go hungry. Stalin took a train east to Siberia in January 1928 and watched, personally, as squads requisitioned grain at gunpoint from villages along the Ob. He came back convinced that the peasantry could not be coaxed, only broken.

The decision was taken in the autumn of 1929. Private farming would end. Twenty-five million peasant households would be merged into collective farms - kolkhozy - which would deliver fixed quotas of grain to the state at prices the state set. The kulaks, the supposedly wealthy peasants who were said to be holding the countryside hostage, would be "liquidated as a class." What that meant in practice was deportation, dispossession, and in tens of thousands of cases, execution.

The word kulak had almost no fixed meaning. A peasant who owned two cows instead of one, who hired a seasonal laborer at harvest, who had a tin roof rather than thatch, could be denounced as a kulak by a neighbor who wanted the cow. Local activists, often urban Communists shipped out to the villages, were given quotas. Three categories: the first to be shot or sent to camps, the second deported to the far north or Kazakhstan, the third resettled on the worst land in their own districts. By 1932, somewhere between five and seven million people had been displaced. Cattle cars rolled north all winter. Children froze on the floors of unheated barracks at the end of the line.

The peasants who remained resisted in the only way they could. They slaughtered their animals rather than hand them to the collectives. Between 1928 and 1933, the Soviet Union lost roughly half of its cattle, two-thirds of its sheep and goats, and most of its horses. Women hid grain under floorboards and in graveyards. Whole villages refused to plant. The authorities answered with searches, beatings, and finally with quotas that exceeded what the land could produce.

By 1932 the procurement targets for Ukraine, the North Caucasus, and Kazakhstan were set so high that meeting them meant taking everything, including the seed grain for the next year's planting. When peasants failed to deliver, brigades came back and took it anyway. In August 1932 a decree made the theft of socialist property - including a handful of wheat picked up in a harvested field - punishable by death or ten years in a camp. Children were shot for gleaning. In November, villages that failed to meet quotas were placed on a "black list": no manufactured goods, no salt, no matches, no kerosene could be sold there. They were sealed off from the rest of the country and left to starve.

What happened in Ukraine in 1932 and 1933 has a Ukrainian name now: the Holodomor, the killing by hunger. Roads out of the famine zone were blocked by internal passport checks introduced in December 1932. Peasants who tried to walk to the cities were turned back. Trains running west through the grain-producing provinces had their blinds drawn so passengers would not see the bodies in the stations. Estimates of the dead vary - historians differ on whether the figure for Ukraine alone is closer to three million or four - and a further million or more died in Kazakhstan, where the forced settlement of nomadic herders destroyed a way of life that had existed for centuries.

Stalin's response, when foreign Communists raised the rumors, was that there was no famine. The harvest of 1933 was officially excellent. The grain exports continued. In 1932 and 1933, while villages along the Dnieper ate bark and grass and, in the worst districts, each other, the Soviet Union sold roughly 3.5 million tons of grain on the world market. By 1934 the resistance was over. The countryside that emerged from collectivization was quieter, poorer, and entirely the state's. It would remain so for the next sixty years.

Industrialization at Breakneck Speed

The grain taken from the villages paid for the factories. That was the logic. Sell wheat abroad, buy German turbines, American tractors, British steel; hire foreign engineers; build, at impossible speed, the heavy industrial base that Russia had never managed under the tsars.

The First Five-Year Plan was announced in 1928 and declared completed, with great ceremony, in four years and three months. The targets had been fantastical from the start - pig iron to triple, electricity to multiply sixfold, coal output to double - and many of them were not in fact reached. The numbers that appeared in *Pravda* were the numbers Moscow needed to print. But the factories themselves were real. Magnitogorsk, an entire city built on the steppe around a single enormous steel combine, rose from nothing between 1929 and 1932. The Dnieper hydroelectric station, the largest in Europe when it opened in 1932, came on line on schedule. The Stalingrad and Kharkov tractor plants, the Gorky automobile works, the new mines of the Kuzbass, the railway extensions across Central Asia - all of it was built, more or less, on the timetable Stalin demanded.

The human cost was extraordinary. Workers were hauled off trains at half-finished construction sites and told to dig foundations in February with no barracks ready. They lived in tents, in mud huts, in holes scraped out of hillsides and roofed with planks. At Magnitogorsk in the first winters, temperatures dropped to forty below and frostbite was so common the medical reports stopped recording minor cases. American engineers who came to advise on the steel mills wrote home in shock at what Russian workers were expected to endure. They also noted that the mills got built.

The workforce expanded by tens of millions in less than a decade, drawn from the dispossessed countryside. Peasants who had lost their farms walked into the cities and were absorbed into the new factories. Women entered industrial labor in numbers no previous society had matched. By 1939 the urban population had nearly doubled. Discipline was savage. A 1932 decree made lateness of more than twenty minutes grounds for dismissal, eviction from factory housing, and loss of ration card. A 1940 decree made it a criminal offense to quit a job without permission. Managers who missed targets were charged with sabotage. Workers who broke machines, even accidentally, could be sent to camps. The slogan was that there were no fortresses Bolsheviks could not storm, and the corollary was that anyone who failed to storm one had chosen, by his failure, to be an enemy.

The system also produced, alongside the terror, a real enthusiasm. Young workers from peasant families were learning to read, operating machinery, drawing wages, climbing into a Soviet middle class that had not existed five years earlier. The shock-worker movement, and after 1935 the Stakhanovite campaign - named for the Donbas miner Alexei Stakhanov, who supposedly cut fourteen times his shift's quota of coal in a single night - turned record-breaking into a national sport. Some of the records were genuine. Many were staged. Either way, the Stakhanovites got medals, apartments, cars, and a place in the newsreels, and millions of workers tried to imitate them.

By 1937 the Soviet Union was producing more steel than France and Britain combined. It had built, in less than a decade, an industrial economy capable of arming the largest land army in the world. When the war came in 1941, the factories beyond the Urals would matter more than anyone in Berlin had imagined. None of it would have been possible without the famine that paid for it, or the camps that fed it labor.

The Great Terror

On December 1, 1934, Sergei Kirov, the party boss of Leningrad and, after Stalin, perhaps the most popular Bolshevik in the country, was shot dead in the corridor outside his office. The assassin was a disgruntled former party member named Leonid Nikolaev. Whether Stalin ordered the killing - historians have argued the question for decades and the documentary record remains incomplete - is less important than what he did with it.

Within hours, a decree was issued allowing the political police to investigate, try, and execute suspects in terrorism cases within ten days, with no defense lawyers, no appeals, and sentences carried out immediately. The Kirov murder became the founding event of a conspiracy that grew, over the next four years, to include essentially every Old Bolshevik, every senior officer in the Red Army, and a substantial part of the Soviet population.

The first show trial opened in August 1936. Zinoviev, Kamenev, and fourteen others stood in the dock and confessed to having organized a "Trotskyite-Zinovievite Terrorist Center" responsible for Kirov's death and for plotting to kill Stalin. They had been broken in the cellars of the Lubyanka by months of interrogation, threats against their families, and promises - never kept - of their lives. All sixteen were shot within twenty-four hours of the verdict. The second trial, in January 1937, took out Pyatakov and the technical intelligentsia who had run the Five-Year Plans. The third, in March 1938, finished Bukharin and Rykov. Each trial widened the alleged conspiracy. Each defendant confessed in court, in detail, to fantastical crimes: poisoning workers, wrecking railways, plotting with German and Japanese intelligence, planning to dismember the Soviet Union and hand pieces to foreign powers. Foreign observers watched in disbelief. The American ambassador, Joseph Davies, reported that the confessions seemed genuine. They were not.

In June 1937, eight senior Red Army commanders, including Marshal Tukhachevsky, the most talented strategist in the Soviet armed forces, were tried in secret and shot the same night. Over the next eighteen months roughly half the officer corps was arrested. Three of the five marshals, thirteen of the fifteen army commanders, fifty of the fifty-seven corps commanders, and 154 of the 186 divisional commanders disappeared. When Hitler attacked in 1941, the Red Army would be led by men who had been captains and majors four years earlier.

The terror reached far beyond the elite. NKVD Order 00447, issued in July 1937, set quotas by region for arrests in two categories: shot, and sent to camps. The quotas were filled, then doubled, then filled again. Local NKVD chiefs requested permission to exceed their numbers and were rarely refused. Engineers, schoolteachers, priests, foreign Communists who had taken refuge in Moscow, Poles, Latvians, Koreans on the Pacific coast, peasants denounced by neighbors, husbands denounced by wives, children who said the wrong thing at school - all flowed into the same machine.

The mechanics were almost banal. A knock at the door, usually after midnight. A search that scattered books and broke furniture. A black car, called a "raven," to take the suspect to a district prison. Interrogation by relays of officers working twelve-hour shifts, while the prisoner stood under bright lights for days. A confession. A signature. A troika - three officials meeting in secret - issuing a sentence in minutes. If shooting, a basement, a single bullet to the back of the head, a pit outside the city. If camp, a transport east.

Between 1937 and 1938 roughly 1.5 million people were arrested on political charges. About 700,000 were shot. The killings ran at an average of around 1,000 per day for the worst eighteen months. Bodies were dumped in mass graves at Butovo outside Moscow, in the forests of Kuropaty near Minsk, in pits across Siberia. Most of the graves would not be found for fifty years.

In late 1938 Stalin called a halt. The head of the NKVD, Nikolai Yezhov, who had run the operation, was himself arrested, tortured, and shot in 1940. His successor, Lavrenty Beria, released a few of the surviving prisoners and announced that excesses had occurred under the previous administration. The terror had achieved what

Stalin wanted. There were no more Old Bolsheviks. There were no more generals who remembered the civil war. There was no one in any position of responsibility who had not been promoted by Stalin personally, and who did not know, in the marrow of his bones, what would happen if he failed.

The Gulag Archipelago

The camps had existed since 1919. Lenin had established the first of them on the Solovetsky Islands, an old monastery in the White Sea where political prisoners were sent to dig peat and freeze. Under Stalin the system swelled into something without precedent: a parallel country of barbed wire, watchtowers, and timber barracks, scattered from the Arctic to the Pacific, administered by a Main Directorate of Corrective Labor Camps whose Russian initials spelled GULAG.

At its peak in the early 1950s the system held roughly 2.5 million prisoners in any given year, and several million more passed through it across the Stalin period. Estimates of total deaths in the camps run between 1.5 and 1.8 million, with many more dying shortly after release from diseases contracted inside. The figures remain contested; the archives are incomplete and historians differ on how to count those who died in transit, in exile settlements, or in special labor colonies that overlapped with the camps proper.

The economic role was deliberate. Prisoners built the White Sea-Baltic Canal in 1931-33, dug for gold at Kolyma in temperatures that froze mercury, cut timber in the forests of Komi, mined nickel at Norilsk, laid the railway to Vorkuta. Whole industries in the far north and east existed because no free worker would have gone there voluntarily. The economists of the Five-Year Plans counted on this labor and built it into their targets.

The conditions varied. A camp in the Moscow region where prisoners assembled radios was survivable; a gold mine in the Kolyma basin in winter, where men worked twelve-hour shifts at fifty below on a ration of frozen bread and watery soup, was very often not. New arrivals at Kolyma in the late 1930s had a life expectancy, by some accounts, of a single winter. The first task of any prisoner was to find indoor work - in the kitchen, the bathhouse, the infirmary, the bookkeeping office - because outdoor labor in the worst camps was a slow sentence of death.

The prisoners were not, mostly, the political enemies of legend. The majority, year by year, were ordinary criminals or peasants convicted under economic statutes - the law on stolen ears of grain, the law against leaving a job, the law against being twenty minutes late. The politicals, sentenced under Article 58 of the criminal code, were a minority, though a famous one. They wrote the memoirs, when they survived. The vast majority of the dead left nothing.

Aleksandr Solzhenitsyn, who would later give the system its name in the West, was arrested in 1945 for jokes about Stalin in letters to a school friend at the front. He served eight years. What he wrote afterward, from the dacha outside Moscow where he typed at night with the curtains drawn, would not be published in his own country until Stalin had been dead for nearly forty years. By then the watchtowers at most of the camps had been pulled down for firewood, and the names of the men buried under the permafrost at Kolyma were known only to their families, if at all.

The watchtowers would come down for firewood and the names under the permafrost would be forgotten by everyone but their families. Before any of that could happen, though, the system that had built the camps had to survive the war it had spent the 1930s preparing for and pretending it would not have to fight. The pact signed in the Kremlin in August 1939 bought time. It did not buy safety. When the trucks crossed the border in June 1941, the country that had been hollowed out by purges and famines discovered what it still had left to give.

Chapter 15
The Great Patriotic War

The Nazi-Soviet Pact and Its Collapse

In August 1939, in a room in the Kremlin, Vyacheslav Molotov and Joachim von Ribbentrop signed a piece of paper that astonished the world. The two states whose ideologies had defined themselves against each other - the homeland of revolutionary communism and the citadel of European fascism - had agreed not to fight. They had also agreed, in secret protocols, to divide the lands between them: Poland, the Baltic states, parts of Romania. Stalin reportedly raised a glass to Hitler's health.

The pact bought Stalin time, and it bought Hitler a free hand in the west. Within days the Wehrmacht crossed into Poland; within weeks Soviet troops crossed in from the east to claim their share. Over the next twenty months the Soviet Union absorbed eastern Poland, the Baltic republics, Bessarabia, and northern Bukovina, and fought a costly winter war against Finland that exposed how poorly its army performed in the field. Stalin used the breathing space to expand industry behind the Urals, to push military production, and to keep promised shipments of grain, oil, and metals flowing west to Germany - trainloads that would, in a matter of months, be turned against him.

Warnings began to arrive in the spring of 1941. They came from Soviet spies in Tokyo and Berlin, from British intelligence, from German deserters slipping across the border, from frontier guards reporting the buildup of armor and aircraft on the other side of the demarcation line in Poland. Richard Sorge, the Soviet agent in Tokyo, gave a date. Winston Churchill sent a personal warning. Stalin ignored them all. He had convinced himself, perhaps because he wanted to be convinced, that Hitler would not open a second front while Britain remained undefeated. He suspected the warnings of being British provocations meant to drag him into the war.

In the early hours of June 22, 1941, the German ambassador delivered a declaration of war to Molotov in Moscow. By then, the bombing had already begun. Three million German soldiers, supported by Romanian, Hungarian, Italian, Finnish, and Slovak troops, were crossing the border on a front that stretched from the Baltic to the Black Sea. It was the largest invasion force ever assembled in the history of war.

Stalin's response, in the first hours, was paralysis. The accounts of what happened in his office that day vary, but the broad picture is consistent: he could not believe it, then he could not act, then he retreated to his dacha at Kuntsevo and refused to come out. For something like ten days, the Soviet Union was a state with no public leader. When Politburo members finally drove out to fetch him on June 30, Stalin is said to have thought they had come to arrest him. Instead they asked him to head a new State Defense Committee. He agreed.

On July 3, he addressed the country by radio. The opening words were not the formula of a Marxist general secretary. They were the words of an Orthodox priest, or a tsar: *Brothers and sisters! I turn to you, my friends.* The war, he told them, was not a war between socialism and fascism. It was a Patriotic War, a war for the survival of the Russian land and the peoples who lived on it. The name stuck. From that moment, in Soviet propaganda and in Soviet memory, this was the Great Patriotic War, the second of its kind, the elder brother to 1812.

The pact was dead. The country was burning. Whole air regiments had been destroyed on the ground in the first morning. By the end of the first week, the German army was four hundred miles inside Soviet territory.

Barbarossa and the Road to Moscow

The Germans came in three army groups. Army Group North drove toward Leningrad through the Baltic states. Army Group Center, the largest and strongest, struck through Belorussia along the old Napoleonic road to Moscow. Army Group South pushed into Ukraine, toward Kiev and the grain fields and the iron and coal of the Donbas. Hitler's directive made clear what the war was for: *Lebensraum*, living space, and the resources to sustain a thousand-year Reich. Ukraine was to feed Germany. The Soviet population, in the Nazi view, was a mass of *Untermenschen* to be killed, starved, deported, or reduced to slave labor.

The first weeks were a catastrophe of a kind no European army had ever experienced. Whole Soviet armies were swallowed in vast encirclements. At Bialystok and Minsk, more than three hundred thousand Soviet soldiers were taken prisoner. At Smolensk, another three hundred thousand. At Kiev, in September, the Germans closed a ring around four Soviet armies and took six hundred and sixty thousand prisoners - the largest single capture of soldiers in the history of warfare. By the end of 1941, German records counted more than three million Soviet prisoners of war. Most of them would not survive. The Wehrmacht had made no provision to feed them, and in many cases no intention to. They died in open fields behind barbed wire, of starvation, of typhus, of cold, of shooting.

Behind the front lines, the killing took another form. Special units called Einsatzgruppen followed the army into the conquered territories with orders to murder Jews, Communist Party officials, Roma, and anyone judged a threat. At Babi Yar, a ravine outside Kiev, more than thirty-three thousand Jews were shot in two days at the end of September. This pattern was repeated in hundreds of towns and villages across the western Soviet Union. The Holocaust by bullets began here, in the summer and autumn of 1941, and the largest mass killings of Jews in the war happened not in the death camps of Poland but in the fields and forests of Ukraine, Belorussia, and the Baltic.

Even as it lost armies, the Soviet state did not collapse. In a feat of organization that has few parallels, more than fifteen hundred factories were disassembled, loaded onto freight trains, and shipped east - to the Urals, to Siberia, to Central Asia - where workers reassembled them on bare ground and began producing tanks and aircraft within months. Whole populations moved with the machines. The Magnitogorsk steelworks ran at full capacity. The T-34 tank, the best medium tank of the war, came off new assembly lines in Chelyabinsk, in Nizhny Tagil, in Sverdlovsk. The Soviet economy, even broken in half, was outproducing Germany in tanks and artillery by 1942.

The Germans kept coming. By October, Army Group Center was within sixty miles of Moscow. Government offices were evacuated to Kuibyshev on the Volga. Lenin's body was taken from the Mausoleum and sent east. Panic broke out in the capital - shops were looted, files were burned in the streets, the diplomatic corps fled. Stalin stayed. On November 7, the anniversary of the Revolution, he reviewed a military parade in Red Square as snow fell and the front rumbled in the distance. The soldiers marched directly from the parade to the front lines.

Then the weather turned. The rains of October had already churned the roads into impassable mud, immobilizing German armor. In November came the cold - first a sharp freeze that hardened the ground and allowed the panzers to move again, then a deeper cold for which the German army had not prepared. Engines would not start. Lubricants congealed. Men in summer uniforms froze in their foxholes. In early December, with the lead German units close enough to see the spires of the Kremlin through binoculars, Marshal Zhukov launched a counteroffensive with fresh divisions brought from Siberia, where Sorge had assured Stalin the Japanese would not attack. The Germans were thrown back a hundred miles from Moscow - the first major defeat the Wehrmacht had suffered in the war.

Stalingrad

By the summer of 1942, Hitler had decided that the way to break the Soviet Union was through its oil. The new offensive, Operation Blue, drove southeast toward the Caucasus and the wells of Baku and Grozny. To protect the flank of this advance, the German Sixth Army under General Friedrich Paulus was sent against a city on the lower Volga that bore Stalin's name.

The Luftwaffe arrived first. On August 23, more than a thousand sorties reduced most of Stalingrad to rubble in a single day. The city's wooden districts burned for a week. Tens of thousands of civilians were killed. The German ground forces reached the suburbs by the end of August, expecting to take the rest in days. They did not. What followed was four months of fighting unlike anything either army had experienced.

The defense of the city fell to General Vasily Chuikov and his 62nd Army. Chuikov understood that the German advantage lay in coordinated combined-arms warfare - tanks, aircraft, and infantry working together in open country. He ordered his men to stay so close to the German lines that the Luftwaffe could not bomb without hitting its own troops. He called this *hugging the enemy*. The fighting moved into factories, apartment blocks, sewers, and staircases. A single building - the Pavlov House, defended by a sergeant and a few dozen men - held out for nearly two months. The grain elevator changed hands repeatedly. The Mamaev Kurgan, the hill at the city's center, was shelled so heavily that the soil turned black and metallic and grew no grass for years afterward.

Soviet soldiers crossed the Volga at night under German artillery to reinforce the city. Many did not make it across. Those who did had a life expectancy, in the front-line units, measured in hours. The 13th Guards Rifle Division lost roughly thirty percent of its men in the first twenty-four hours after crossing. Yet the line held. Snipers became famous on both sides. Vasily Zaitsev, a young man from the Urals who had hunted in the taiga as a boy, was credited with more than two hundred kills and turned into a propaganda figure.

While Paulus's army ground itself to pieces in the city, the Soviet General Staff was planning something larger. Zhukov and Vasilevsky had noticed that the long flanks of the German advance, north and south of Stalingrad, were held not by Germans but by less well-equipped Romanian, Italian, and Hungarian armies. On November 19, in a blizzard, the Red Army launched Operation Uranus - two great pincer movements that crashed through the flank armies and met four days later at the town of Kalach, west of Stalingrad. The German Sixth Army was encircled. Three hundred thousand men were trapped inside the pocket.

Hitler forbade Paulus to break out. Hermann Goering promised that the Luftwaffe would supply the army by air. It could not. The daily tonnage required was several times what the transport fleet could deliver, and Soviet fighters and anti-aircraft fire bled the supply effort to death. Inside the pocket, German soldiers ate their horses, then their dogs. Frostbite, typhus, and starvation killed thousands. A relief column under Manstein got within thirty miles of the city before it was stopped.

On January 31, 1943, Paulus surrendered. He had been promoted to field marshal the day before; Hitler had pointed out that no German field marshal had ever been taken alive. Paulus did not take the hint. Two days later, the last pockets of resistance in the northern factories surrendered as well. Of the roughly three hundred thousand men encircled, fewer than ninety-one thousand were still alive to be marched off as prisoners. Of those, perhaps five thousand ever saw Germany again.

In Berlin, the radio played funeral music for three days. In London, Churchill ordered the bells of Westminster Abbey rung. The historian Geoffrey Roberts and others have argued that what happened on the Volga in those four months did more than any other event to decide the outcome of the war. The Germans would never again hold the strategic initiative on the Eastern Front. The Soviet Union, having absorbed the worst blow ever struck against a modern state, was now advancing.

While Stalingrad was being fought house by house, another city eight hundred miles to the north was dying slowly. The siege of Leningrad began on September 8, 1941, when German forces severed the last land connection to the rest of the country. Hitler had decided not to storm the city. He intended to starve it.

Before the war, Leningrad held about three million people. The encirclement happened so quickly that few could be evacuated, and the food stores in the city were modest - some of them lost in a German bombing raid in early September that destroyed the Badaev warehouses. By November, the bread ration for non-working civilians was down to 125 grams a day, about four slices, made of flour cut with sawdust and cellulose. People ate wallpaper paste for the flour in it. They boiled leather belts. They ate cats, then dogs, then rats, then nothing. In the worst months, the dead lay in the streets and stairwells because no one had the strength to bury them. A diary kept by a schoolgirl named Tanya Savicheva recorded her family's deaths one by one in a small notebook: *Mama died May 13. Savichevs died. All died. Only Tanya left.*

The winter of 1941 to 1942 was the worst. Temperatures dropped to forty below. The city had no heating, no electricity, no running water. People hauled water from holes cut in the Neva. The death rate in January and February reached something like a hundred thousand a month, and estimates of the total civilian dead during the siege range from six hundred thousand to over a million.

The city did not surrender. Factories kept working - the Kirov Plant continued producing tanks within range of German guns. Composers composed. Dmitri Shostakovich wrote the first three movements of his Seventh Symphony in Leningrad during the bombing and finished it in evacuation. In August 1942, an orchestra of starving and half-dead musicians performed it in the besieged city. Soviet artillery laid down a barrage to keep the Germans quiet for the duration of the concert. The broadcast was beamed out by loudspeaker so the German lines could hear it.

A lifeline ran across Lake Ladoga - the Road of Life. In summer, barges. In winter, when the ice was thick enough, trucks. They brought in flour and ammunition and carried out the weakest of the population. Drivers froze at the wheel. Trucks went through the ice. But the road kept moving. In January 1943, Soviet forces opened a narrow corridor along the southern shore of the lake, restoring rail connection. The siege itself was not fully lifted until January 27, 1944 - 872 days after it had begun.

When relief came, much of the city was still standing, in its way. The Hermitage had hidden its paintings in the cellars. The bronze horsemen had been buried under sand. The starved survivors who came out into the streets that January found a city that had lost more people in a single siege than the combined wartime losses of the United States and the British Empire. They did not call themselves heroes. They called themselves Leningraders. The word, after that, meant something it had not meant before.

To Berlin and Beyond

In the summer of 1943, the Germans tried one more time. At Kursk, in July, they launched a great pincer attack against a Soviet salient bulging into their lines. The Red Army had been warned by intelligence and had spent months preparing - laying minefields, digging anti-tank ditches, building defensive belts in depth. The German offensive ran into the deepest prepared defensive position in the history of warfare and was ground down. The tank battle at Prokhorovka, on July 12, pitted hundreds of T-34s against Tigers and Panthers in a single afternoon of close-range fighting. After Kursk, the Germans never mounted another strategic offensive in the east.

From then on, the war moved west. The Red Army that pushed back across the Dnieper in late 1943 was a different army than the one shattered in 1941. Its officers, the survivors of two years of catastrophic schooling, knew how to coordinate armor and infantry and artillery on a scale the Germans could no longer match. Soviet industry was producing more tanks, more aircraft, more artillery than Germany and all its satellites combined. American Lend-Lease - jeeps, trucks, locomotives, canned meat, aviation fuel - kept the Soviet army mobile. The trucks were what moved the offensives. The men were what won the battles.

In June 1944, days after the Western Allies landed in Normandy, the Soviets launched Operation Bagration in Belorussia. It was timed, and named, and intended as the larger blow. Within five weeks, Army Group Center - the same force that had advanced on Moscow three years before - ceased to exist. Twenty-eight German divisions were destroyed. Soviet soldiers stood on the Vistula, across the river from Warsaw. They watched while the Polish Home Army rose against the Germans inside the city and was annihilated. The Red Army did not move. Whether Stalin held back for military reasons or political ones - the Home Army was loyal to the Polish government in London, not to Moscow - historians still differ.

Through the autumn and winter the offensives continued. Romania, Bulgaria, Hungary, Yugoslavia - one by one the German allies in eastern Europe fell or switched sides. Budapest was taken after a brutal siege. Vienna fell in April. The Soviet armies that closed on Berlin in the spring of 1945 numbered over two million men. The final assault began on April 16. The fighting in the streets of Berlin matched anything the Eastern Front had produced; tens of thousands of soldiers and civilians died in the last two weeks of the war. On April 30, Hitler shot himself in his bunker. On May 2, the Berlin garrison surrendered. On the night of May 8 to 9, in a German army engineering school in the Berlin suburb of Karlshorst, Field Marshal Wilhelm Keitel signed the unconditional surrender of all German forces.

The figures, when they were finally counted, did not feel like figures. Twenty-seven million Soviet citizens dead, of whom perhaps two-thirds were civilians. Seventeen hundred towns and seventy thousand villages destroyed. Whole national populations deported - Chechens, Crimean Tatars, Volga Germans, Kalmyks - on Stalin's orders, accused collectively of disloyalty. The country that had won the war was, in many places, no longer a country but a terrain of foundations and chimneys.

In June 1945, a victory parade was held in Red Square. Rain fell. Soviet soldiers carried captured German standards to the foot of Lenin's Mausoleum and threw them down in a pile on the wet stones. Stalin stood above them and watched. He did not speak. He did not need to. Behind him, the empire he now ruled stretched from the Elbe to the Pacific, and from the Arctic to the borders of Iran. In front of him, the standards lay in the rain.

The standards lay in the rain on Red Square and Stalin watched without speaking. The empire he now ruled stretched from the Elbe to the Pacific, and the price of building it had been paid in a generation of dead. What he did with that empire in the years that remained to him, and what his successors did with it once he was gone, would define the second half of the twentieth century for half the world. The wartime alliance had not yet quite ended. The next argument, the one that would last forty years, had not yet quite begun.

Chapter 16
Superpower and Thaw

The Iron Curtain Descends

In the summer of 1945, Soviet soldiers were still finding bodies in the cellars of Berlin. They were also stripping factories. Whole assembly lines, lathes, rolling mills, even sections of railway track were being crated up and sent east, repayment in kind for what Germany had done to Belorussia and Ukraine. The Red Army had arrived as a liberating force in some places and an occupying one in others, and in many places it was both at once. By the time the boots stopped moving, they had stopped along a line that ran from the Baltic down through central Germany and into the Balkans. That line would harden.

Stalin did not need a master plan to build an empire in Eastern Europe. He needed only the army that was already there. In Poland, Romania, Bulgaria, Hungary, and the Soviet zone of Germany, local communists - many of them returning from Moscow exile - were folded into coalition governments. Within three or four years, those coalitions had shed everyone who was not a communist. Elections were arranged. Opposition leaders fled or disappeared. Czechoslovakia, which had tried to keep a foot in both camps, fell into line in February 1948 after a coup in Prague.

The Western response came in two pieces. The first was rhetorical. Winston Churchill, out of office and speaking at a small college in Fulton, Missouri in March 1946, said that an iron curtain had descended across the continent from Stettin in the Baltic to Trieste in the Adriatic. The phrase stuck because it was true. The second piece was material. The United States, which had emerged from the war with an intact industrial base and a monopoly on the atomic bomb, began pouring money into Western Europe through the

Marshall Plan. Stalin forbade the countries under his control from accepting it. The split was now economic as well as military.

In 1948 the Soviets blockaded the western sectors of Berlin, hoping to squeeze the Americans, British, and French out of the city. Instead, the Allies flew in coal and flour for almost a year, a plane landing every few minutes at Tempelhof. Stalin lifted the blockade in May 1949. That same year, NATO was founded. A few months later, in August, the Soviet Union detonated its first atomic bomb, years earlier than American intelligence had predicted. The monopoly was over.

By the end of 1949 the map of postwar Europe was set, and the rest of the world was beginning to be drawn into the same pattern. In October, Mao Zedong proclaimed the People's Republic of China. The following June, North Korean troops crossed the 38th parallel into the south, armed with Soviet equipment and operating with Stalin's grudging permission. American and Chinese soldiers were soon killing each other in the mountains around the Yalu River. Stalin, who had encouraged the war from a safe distance, kept Soviet pilots flying over Korea in unmarked MiGs.

The world had organized itself, almost without anyone deciding to, into two camps. Embassies in Moscow filed reports about food shortages and parade routes. In Washington, a State Department official named George Kennan had already laid out the logic of what would be called containment: the Soviet Union was an ideological adversary that would press wherever it met no resistance and recede wherever it did. For the next forty years, that was the assumption almost every American policy would rest on. And for the next four years, the man on the other side of the table remained the same: an aging, suspicious Georgian who slept badly and worked through the night.

Stalin in his seventies was not a man anyone wanted to be alone in a room with. He had moved most of his life to a dacha at Kuntsevo, outside Moscow, where he ate late and drank with a small circle of subordinates who were terrified of him and of each other. Photographs from the period show a thickset old man with yellow teeth and a tired face. The pockmarks from his childhood smallpox had deepened. His left arm, withered since boyhood, he kept tucked.

The terror had not ended with the war. It had simply slowed and changed targets. Returning prisoners of war were sifted; many went straight from German camps to Soviet ones, suspected of having been turned or simply of having seen too much of the West. Whole nationalities had been deported during the war - Chechens, Crimean Tatars, Volga Germans, Kalmyks - and they remained in Central Asian exile. In 1948 a campaign against "rootless cosmopolitans" began, a barely coded attack on Soviet Jews. The Yiddish actor Solomon Mikhoels was murdered in Minsk that January by the secret police, in a killing staged to look like a traffic accident. The Jewish Anti-Fascist Committee, which Mikhoels had led, was shut down, and its leading members were shot in 1952 after a closed trial.

Inside the party, the postwar years brought the Leningrad Affair, in which a generation of younger officials who had run the city during the siege were arrested and executed on invented charges of conspiracy. Andrei Zhdanov, who had been the chief enforcer of cultural orthodoxy, died in 1948, and his clients were purged after him. The men who survived around Stalin - Beria, Malenkov, Molotov, Khrushchev, Bulganin - watched one another and watched the boss, and waited.

By the winter of 1952 Stalin was talking openly about a new wave of arrests. In January 1953, *Pravda* announced the discovery of a "Doctors' Plot": a group of mostly Jewish Kremlin physicians had supposedly been poisoning the leadership on behalf of foreign intelligence. Arrests began. Rumors spread that mass deportations of Soviet Jews were being prepared. The atmosphere in Moscow resembled 1937. Then, on the night of March 1, Stalin had a stroke at Kuntsevo. His guards, afraid to enter his quarters without being summoned, did not check on him for hours. When his subordinates arrived they hesitated to call doctors, because the best Kremlin doctors were already in prison. He died on March 5.

The reaction in the country was extraordinary. Crowds in Moscow surged toward the Hall of Columns to see the body, and people were trampled to death in the streets. Citizens who had lost husbands and brothers to the camps wept anyway. He had been the only leader most of them could remember. In the corridors of the Kremlin, the surviving members of the Politburo divided the offices among themselves with surprising speed. Lavrenti Beria, the head of the secret police, was the most feared. Within weeks he was releasing prisoners and floating reforms - perhaps trying to position himself as a liberator, perhaps just trying to survive. He miscalculated. In June his colleagues had him arrested at a Kremlin meeting. He was tried in secret and shot in December.

The struggle that followed was quieter, conducted through committee votes and provincial appointments rather than gunfire. By 1955 the man who had emerged on top was the one most of his rivals had underestimated: a short, balding Ukrainian peasant's son with a habit of speaking too loudly.

The Secret Speech

On the night of February 25, 1956, the delegates to the Twentieth Congress of the Communist Party of the Soviet Union were summoned back to the hall after the official agenda had ended. Foreign communists were not invited. The doors were closed. Khrushchev climbed to the rostrum and spoke for nearly four hours.

What he said had never been said in that room before. He said that Stalin had built around himself a cult of personality that had no place in a Marxist movement. He said that Stalin had killed loyal communists by the thousands on fabricated charges. He read out the names of Central Committee members elected at the Seventeenth Congress in 1934 and noted how many of them had been shot in the years afterward. He described how confessions had been beaten out of old Bolsheviks. He recounted Stalin's paralysis in the first days of the German invasion, when the leader had retreated to his dacha and refused to speak, leaving the country without direction while Wehrmacht columns rolled toward Minsk and Smolensk. He described Stalin planning military operations on a globe, ignoring his generals, costing lives.

The hall was silent. Some delegates fainted. Others wept. A few, according to later accounts, suffered heart attacks in the days that followed. Khrushchev did not denounce the system itself. Collectivization was not on trial. The Gulag was not on trial. The Party, which he was now leading, was presented as the victim of one man's pathology rather than the architect of an apparatus that had crushed millions. He said nothing about Ukraine in 1933. He said nothing about the deported nationalities. He said almost nothing about the years before 1934, when he himself had been climbing the ladder. The terror, in his telling, began when it began to consume the Party's own.

The speech was secret only in the sense that the Western press was not in the room. Within days, copies were being read aloud at closed Party meetings across the Soviet Union. A text reached the Polish communists, and from there found its way to Israeli intelligence, and from there to the Americans. By June the State Department had published it. Ambassador Charles Bohlen, who had served in Moscow under Stalin and now read the speech in translation, understood at once that something fundamental had shifted. The men who ran the Soviet Union were now on record acknowledging that their predecessor had been a murderer.

The consequences came quickly and not where Khrushchev wanted them. In Poland that summer, workers in Poznan went on strike and were fired on by their own government. A new leadership took over in Warsaw, one that Moscow tolerated only after Khrushchev flew in and shouted himself hoarse. In Hungary, the unrest went further. Crowds in Budapest pulled down a giant statue of Stalin in October. A reformist government under Imre Nagy announced that Hungary would leave the Warsaw Pact. Soviet tanks rolled into the city in early November and crushed the rising street by street. Thousands of Hungarians were killed. Nagy was arrested under a promise of safe passage, held for nearly two years, and hanged in 1958.

De-Stalinization had limits, and the limits were drawn in blood. Inside the Soviet Union, though, something had changed that could not be put back. Prisoners began returning from the camps in larger numbers. Writers tested what could now be written. A young provincial schoolteacher named Alexander Solzhenitsyn, released after eight years in the system, began drafting a short novel about a single day in a labor camp. He would publish it, with Khrushchev's personal permission, in 1962. The book ended with the prisoner Ivan Denisovich falling asleep, almost content, because nothing especially bad had happened that day. There were 3,653 days like that in his sentence.

Sputnik, Gagarin, and the Cosmos

On the night of October 4, 1957, amateur radio operators around the world picked up a steady beeping signal on a frequency of 20.005 megahertz. The source was a polished metal sphere about the size of a beach ball, with four whip antennas, orbiting the Earth every ninety-six minutes at an altitude of several hundred kilometers. The Soviets called it Sputnik, which simply means traveling companion. It had been launched from a desert site in Kazakhstan called Baikonur, on a rocket originally designed to carry a hydrogen bomb to North America.

For the United States, Sputnik was a shock that took weeks to absorb. American newspapers had spent the early 1950s describing Soviet technology as derivative and clunky. Now there was a Soviet machine passing over Kansas every hour and a half, and there was no American machine to answer it. A first U.S. attempt in December 1957, the Vanguard rocket, exploded on the launchpad while television cameras watched. The press called it Flopnik. The shock produced a hurried reorganization of American science education, the founding of NASA in 1958, and an unprecedented expansion of federal money for universities. For Khrushchev the propaganda value was almost more important than the technology. Here was proof, broadcast in radio pulses, that a country devastated only twelve years earlier had overtaken the Americans in the most visible competition imaginable. A month after Sputnik, the Soviets launched a second satellite carrying a dog named Laika. She died in orbit, probably within hours, from overheating, though the Soviets did not say so for decades.

The man behind the rockets was Sergei Korolev, the chief designer, whose name was a state secret for as long as he lived. Korolev had spent six years in the Gulag during the 1930s, part of it in the Kolyma gold fields. He had lost most of his teeth to scurvy. He had been beaten so badly during interrogation that his jaw never set right. He had then been transferred to a *sharashka*, a prison design bureau, and put to work on aircraft. After the war he was given the captured German V-2 rocket as a starting point and told to build something better. He did.

On the morning of April 12, 1961, one of Korolev's rockets lifted a small spherical capsule into orbit. Inside it sat a twenty-seven-year-old air force lieutenant named Yuri Gagarin, the son of a carpenter and a milkmaid from a village west of Moscow. Gagarin orbited the Earth once, in 108 minutes, and parachuted to a field in the Saratov region where a farm woman and her granddaughter watched a man in an orange suit come down out of the sky and asked him if he had come from outer space. He said that he had, and that he was a Soviet citizen, and could they help him find a telephone.

Gagarin became, almost overnight, the most famous man in the world. He had the right face for it, an open Russian face that smiled easily. He was sent on tours of Cuba, Brazil, Britain, Japan. The

British queen had him to lunch. In photographs from those years he looks slightly bewildered by what has happened to him. He went back to flying, and in 1968 was killed when his MiG-15 trainer crashed in fog north of Moscow, at the age of thirty-four. The cause of the crash has never been settled.

The space program was the brightest face of the Khrushchev years. It suggested, briefly, that the system worked - that the long sacrifice of the 1930s and 1940s had bought something more than tanks.

Cuba, Crisis, and Khrushchev's Fall

In April 1961, the same month Gagarin orbited the Earth, a brigade of Cuban exiles trained by the CIA landed at the Bay of Pigs and was destroyed within three days. Fidel Castro, who had taken power two years earlier, was now openly aligning his island with Moscow. For Khrushchev, this was an opening of a kind that had never existed before: a friendly socialist government ninety miles from Florida.

In the summer of 1962, Soviet ships began moving medium-range ballistic missiles to Cuba under tarpaulins. Khrushchev's reasoning was a mix of motives. The Americans had recently stationed Jupiter missiles in Turkey, close enough to Soviet cities to make Moscow nervous. Putting Soviet missiles in Cuba would even the score. It would also protect Castro from another American invasion, which Khrushchev believed was coming. And it would, he hoped, be presented to Washington as a fait accompli after the November midterm elections.

The Americans found the missile sites first, in U-2 photographs taken on October 14. President Kennedy went on television a week later and announced a naval blockade of Cuba, which he carefully called a quarantine because blockade was an act of war. For thirteen days, Soviet and American forces moved closer to nuclear conflict than they ever had before or have since. Submarine captains in the Atlantic were operating out of contact with

Moscow. One Soviet submarine commander, harassed by American destroyers dropping practice depth charges, came within a single vote of his officers of launching a nuclear torpedo. The vote went the other way because of one man, Vasili Arkhipov, whose name was unknown for decades.

The crisis ended in a deal that was partly public and partly secret. Publicly, Khrushchev agreed to remove the missiles in exchange for an American pledge not to invade Cuba. Privately, Kennedy agreed to remove the Jupiter missiles from Turkey a few months later. The secrecy of the second half of the bargain meant that the Soviets appeared, to the world and to their own military, to have backed down without getting anything in return.

That perception cost Khrushchev. The Soviet military had already disliked him for his cuts to conventional forces in favor of missiles, his erratic management, his shouting matches. Party officials disliked him for his constant reorganizations, which threatened their jobs. His agricultural campaigns - the virgin lands scheme in Kazakhstan, the obsession with maize, which he had seen growing in Iowa and tried to plant in places where it could not survive - had produced poor harvests and, by 1963, the embarrassment of importing wheat from Canada. He had quarreled with Mao and split the world communist movement. He had threatened the West with shoes and missiles and then pulled back.

In October 1964, while Khrushchev was on holiday at the Black Sea, his colleagues in the Presidium voted to remove him. He was summoned back to Moscow. The meeting was unpleasant but not violent. Leonid Brezhnev, his protege, read out the charges: voluntarism, hare-brained scheming, rudeness, the cult of his own personality. Khrushchev defended himself briefly and then signed the letter of resignation they had prepared.

He was given a pension, a dacha, a car, and a guard, and told to stay away from politics. He spent his last years dictating memoirs into a tape recorder, walking in his garden, and being ignored by the press he had once dominated. When he died in 1971, *Pravda* printed a single line. His family buried him at Novodevichy

Cemetery in Moscow. The sculptor Ernst Neizvestny - with whom Khrushchev had once publicly quarreled over modern art at an exhibition in 1962 - designed the headstone. It is made of interlocking blocks of black and white marble, and in the niche between them sits a bronze head of Khrushchev, looking out at nothing in particular.

The headstone at Novodevichy was black and white, interlocking, and Khrushchev's bronze head looked out at nothing in particular. The man who had denounced Stalin and pounded his shoe at the United Nations had been retired into silence by colleagues who had decided that there had been enough surprises for one generation. What they wanted was quiet. What they got, for almost two decades, was a country that seemed on the surface to have achieved exactly that, and underneath was slowly running down in ways that the men in the medals on the reviewing stand could not, or would not, see.

Chapter 17
The Long Stagnation

Brezhnev and Developed Socialism

Leonid Brezhnev liked medals. By the end of his life he had collected so many that they could not all fit on his jacket, and the jokes about this were told quietly in apartment kitchens from Riga to Vladivostok. He had four Hero of the Soviet Union stars. He had the Order of Victory, awarded to him in 1978 for a war he had spent as a political commissar of middling rank. He gave himself the Lenin Prize for Literature for a ghostwritten memoir that almost no one read and that everyone, for a time, was required to study.

The medals were the surface. Beneath them sat a country that had stopped pretending it was going somewhere and had started, instead, to insist that it had arrived.

Khrushchev, before his colleagues pushed him out in October 1964, had promised that the Soviet Union would reach full communism by 1980. Apartments for everyone. Abundance. The withering away of money. Brezhnev's circle quietly buried the promise. In its place they put a more modest formula: "developed socialism." The phrase was deliberately flat. It did not commit to a date. It did not commit to abundance. It said only that what existed was, in its way, the thing itself - that the long march had reached a plateau, and that the plateau was where the Soviet people would live.

For a while the plateau was comfortable. Oil prices climbed through the 1970s, and the great Siberian fields at Samotlor and Urengoy poured out hard currency that paid for Canadian wheat and West German pipes and East German consumer goods. Real wages rose. The two-room apartment, the refrigerator, the television, the dacha plot of six hundred square meters - these became available to a generation that remembered communal hallways and rationed bread. The Soviet middle class, if the term fits, was born under Brezhnev. It learned to want things, to queue for them, to know somebody who knew somebody who could get them.

What it did not learn to do was work harder. The factories met their plans by producing what was easy to count rather than what was needed. Tractors were built and abandoned in fields because spare parts never arrived. Shoes were manufactured by the millions in sizes no one wore. The figures climbed every year in the central statistical reports, and the shelves in the provincial stores stayed empty, and everyone above the age of twelve understood that both things were true at once.

Brezhnev himself was not a cruel man, which made him a relief after Stalin and an irritation after Khrushchev. He liked hunting, fast cars, and the company of old comrades. He distrusted change. The phrase he used most often in Politburo meetings was "stability of cadres" - meaning, leave people where they are. Provincial bosses kept their fiefs for twenty years. Ministers grew old in their ministries. The average age of the Politburo crept past seventy. Decisions were postponed, then postponed again, then quietly forgotten. The KGB under Yuri Andropov grew more sophisticated and more pervasive, but it executed almost no one. It preferred psychiatric hospitals, exile, the loss of a job, the quiet word to a wife's employer. The terror had become administrative.

Foreign visitors who came in the early 1970s often left impressed. Moscow's metro ran on time. The streets were clean. Soldiers paraded in Red Square in perfect rows. The Soviet Union had reached strategic parity with the United States, had signed arms control agreements, had a friendly regime in Hanoi and another in Havana and a growing list of allies in Africa. By any measure of power that could be photographed, it had never stood higher. What could not be photographed was harder to see. The country was running on stored fuel, and no one was refilling the tank.

Prague Spring and Its Suppression

In January 1968, the Czechoslovak Communist Party chose a new first secretary, a forty-six-year-old Slovak named Alexander Dubček. He was a lifelong Party man. He had grown up partly in the Soviet Union. He spoke Russian fluently and he believed, sincerely, that the system he served could be made better.

What followed was not a revolution. It was a thaw inside the apparatus. Censorship was relaxed, then in March suspended outright. Newspapers began to print what their editors actually thought. The travel restrictions softened. A government commission opened the files on the show trials of the 1950s. In April the Party published an "Action Program" promising what its authors called socialism with a human face - the rule of law, freedom of assembly, federal status for Slovakia, market mechanisms within a planned economy. The streets of Prague filled with people reading newspapers aloud to one another in the cafes.

From Moscow, it looked different. Brezhnev and his colleagues watched the Czech press attack figures the Soviets considered untouchable. They watched workers' councils form in factories and wondered whether they were soviets or something worse. They remembered Hungary in 1956, when reform inside the Party had escalated, within weeks, into a country trying to leave the Warsaw Pact. They summoned Dubček to meetings in Dresden, in Warsaw, in Čierna nad Tisou on the Slovak-Soviet border. Brezhnev kissed him on both cheeks and warned him. Dubček promised to maintain control and went home and lost control a little further.

On the night of August 20, 1968, the armies of the Soviet Union, Poland, Hungary, Bulgaria, and East Germany crossed the Czechoslovak frontier. By morning, half a million soldiers and several thousand tanks were inside the country. There was no battle. The Czechoslovak army stayed in its barracks under orders. The fighting consisted of unarmed civilians arguing with tank crews in Wenceslas Square, of young men climbing onto T-55s to paint over their numbers, of street signs being turned around or torn down so that the invaders could not find the radio stations.

About a hundred Czechs and Slovaks died. Dubček and the other leaders were arrested, flown to Moscow in handcuffs, kept awake, and after four days of what was officially called negotiation signed a protocol agreeing to the stationing of Soviet troops, the rollback of reforms, and the dismissal of the men they had appointed. Dubček returned to Prague, gave a broken speech on the radio in which he wept audibly, and was kept on as a figurehead for a few months before being demoted to ambassador to Turkey and then to a job in the Slovak forestry service.

In November, at a Party congress in Warsaw, Brezhnev gave the speech that took his name. The sovereignty of socialist states, he said, could not be set against the interests of socialism as a whole. When forces hostile to socialism threatened the development of a socialist country, it was the duty of the other socialist countries to intervene. This was the Brezhnev Doctrine. It did not invent the practice - Hungary in 1956 had done that - but it gave it a sentence anyone could memorize.

The doctrine worked, in the narrow sense. Eastern Europe stayed inside the Soviet bloc for another twenty-one years. But something had broken that August in Prague that could not be repaired. The young Communists of Western Europe, who had defended the Soviet Union through Hungary and the trials and the camps, walked away in disgust. The reform Communists inside the Soviet bloc went silent or went underground. The argument that socialism might be made humane from within the Party was, after August 1968, no longer available to honest people. Anyone who still believed in change had to look outside the Party. Many of them did.

Dissidents: Sakharov, Solzhenitsyn, and the Samizdat

In a small apartment on Chkalov Street in Moscow, a woman sat at a typewriter with five sheets of paper interleaved with four sheets of carbon. She typed slowly and hard, hitting the keys with more force than was comfortable, because the fifth carbon copy was almost unreadable and the people waiting for it had been waiting for weeks. When she finished a page she stacked it face down. When she finished the text she would separate the copies, give four of them away, keep one, and burn the carbons in the kitchen sink.

This was samizdat - *sam-*, self, *-izdat*, publishing house. Self-published. The word was a joke on Gosizdat, the State Publishing House, which printed approved books in editions of a hundred thousand. Samizdat printed unapproved books in editions of five. Then the five were retyped, and each of those was retyped, and so on, until a poem by Mandelstam or a novel by Bulgakov or a transcript of a political trial reached, by geometric multiplication, tens of thousands of readers who would never see their names on a title page. The samizdat world had its own newspaper, the *Chronicle of Current Events*, which began appearing in April 1968 and would run for fifteen years. Its tone was deliberately dry. It reported arrests, trials, sentences, the conditions in the camps, the whereabouts of prisoners, with the affectless precision of a wire service. Its editors were arrested one after another, and each time someone else took over, and the issues kept coming.

Two men became, against their wishes, the public faces of this underground world.

Andrei Sakharov was the father of the Soviet hydrogen bomb. He had three Hero of Socialist Labor stars, the highest scientific honors the state could bestow, and a special apartment, and a car, and the security clearances that came with knowing how to build a thermonuclear weapon. In 1968 he wrote an essay called *Reflections on Progress, Peaceful Coexistence, and Intellectual Freedom.* It argued that the United States and the Soviet Union would have to converge - that capitalism would have to absorb social planning and socialism would have to absorb democratic freedoms - or both would destroy themselves. He sent it through samizdat. It was published in the West in July. He lost his clearances within weeks. For the next decade he wrote letters, gave interviews to foreign correspondents, attended trials, defended Crimean Tatars and Pentecostalists and Jewish refuseniks. In 1975 he received the Nobel Peace Prize. He was not allowed to travel to Oslo. His wife, Elena Bonner, read his speech for him. In January 1980, after he condemned the invasion of Afghanistan, he was arrested without trial and sent into internal exile in Gorky, a city closed to foreigners, where he would remain for almost seven years.

Alexander Solzhenitsyn was something else. He had been a captain of artillery in the Red Army, had been arrested in 1945 for criticizing Stalin in a letter to a friend, had spent eight years in the camps and three more in exile. In 1962 Khrushchev personally authorized the publication of his short novel *One Day in the Life of Ivan Denisovich*, the first description of the Gulag printed in the Soviet Union. Under Brezhnev the door closed again. Solzhenitsyn went on writing. *The First Circle* and *Cancer Ward* circulated in samizdat and were smuggled abroad. In 1970 he won the Nobel Prize for Literature and declined to travel to Stockholm for fear he would not be let back in. Then, between 1958 and 1968, in secret, he wrote *The Gulag Archipelago*: a three-volume forensic history of the Soviet camp system, built from the testimony of 227 former prisoners. He hid the manuscript in pieces with friends across the country. In September 1973 the KGB seized one of the copies from a typist named Elizaveta Voronyanskaya, who hanged herself a few days later. Solzhenitsyn ordered publication in Paris. The first volume appeared in December. In February 1974 he was arrested, stripped of his citizenship, and put on a plane to Frankfurt.

Most dissidents were neither famous physicists nor Nobel laureates. They were schoolteachers, engineers, junior researchers, priests, Baptists, Crimean Tatars, Lithuanian Catholics, Ukrainian nationalists, Jews denied exit visas. They were sentenced under Article 70 (anti-Soviet agitation) or Article 190-1 (spreading slanderous fabrications about the Soviet system) to terms of three, five, seven years in strict-regime camps, often followed by exile. Some were declared insane and held in Serbsky Institute and similar places, dosed with sulfazine and haloperidol, kept until they recanted or could no longer speak in sentences.

None of this would have brought down the Soviet Union by itself. The dissidents were a few thousand people in a country of two hundred and fifty million. But the carbon copies kept moving from hand to hand, and the foreign radio broadcasts kept reading them back into the country in Russian and Ukrainian and Estonian and Georgian, and the people who listened in their kitchens with the volume low began, slowly, to lose the habit of belief.

Afghanistan: The Soviet Vietnam

On the evening of December 27, 1979, a column of Soviet special forces, dressed in Afghan uniforms, drove through the streets of Kabul toward the Tajbeg Palace. Inside the palace, the Afghan president, Hafizullah Amin, was being treated for food poisoning after a lunch arranged, it was later said, by his Soviet cook. The KGB unit broke through the palace gates with armored vehicles, killed the guards, fought their way up the staircases, and shot Amin in his underwear behind the bar in his office. By dawn, Babrak Karmal, a more reliable Afghan Communist, was being installed in his place. Soviet motor rifle divisions were crossing the Amu Darya at Termez and rolling south down the highways toward Herat and Kandahar.

The Politburo had argued about Afghanistan for most of 1979. Andropov of the KGB was for intervention. Ustinov of Defense was for it. Gromyko of the Foreign Ministry came around. The chief of the General Staff, Marshal Ogarkov, was openly against it and was told to be quiet. The argument that won was simple: a friendly Communist regime on the southern border was failing, the Americans had just lost Iran, and a quick decapitating strike would replace one leader with another and the Soviet troops would be home within a year. The first part worked. The second did not.

Afghanistan had a population of about fifteen million. Roughly eighty percent of them lived in villages of mud-brick houses connected to nothing. They were Pashtuns and Tajiks and Uzbeks and Hazaras and Turkmens, divided by language and sect and clan, united in their dislike of being told what to do by men from elsewhere. The Communist government in Kabul had spent the previous eighteen months trying to impose land reform, female literacy, and the abolition of the bride price on people who responded by killing the teachers and the surveyors and burning the schools. The Soviet army arrived to defend a regime the countryside was already at war with.

The army that arrived was built to fight on the North German Plain. It had tanks, armored personnel carriers, motorized infantry, massed artillery. It had conscripts from Ukraine and Belarus and the Baltics who had been trained for eighteen months to repel a NATO assault on Fulda. Some of them had never seen a mountain. They were now expected to garrison a country the size of Texas in which the highest peaks rose above twenty thousand feet, in which the roads ran through gorges where a hundred men with rifles could pin down a battalion for a day, in which every man over the age of twelve owned a weapon or could borrow one.

The mujahideen learned quickly. They mined the roads. They struck convoys and disappeared into the mountains. They were supplied through Pakistan with weapons paid for by the United States, Saudi Arabia, and China - Egyptian-made Kalashnikovs at first, then American-made Stinger anti-aircraft missiles from 1986 onward, which began to knock Soviet helicopters out of the sky and changed the arithmetic of the war.

The Fortieth Army never lost a major engagement. It also never controlled the countryside. It held the cities, the airfields, the main roads in the daytime, and at night it stayed in its bases while the mujahideen moved. By the time the last Soviet soldier crossed back over the Friendship Bridge at Termez in February 1989, around fifteen thousand Soviet servicemen were dead, around fifty thousand wounded, and somewhere between half a million and a million Afghans had been killed.

What came home with the survivors was something the Soviet state had not budgeted for. The veterans were called *Afgantsy*. They drank. They had nightmares. They had a heroin habit picked up in Kandahar that they brought back to Sverdlovsk and Donetsk. They knew, in a way that the newspapers and the television had not told their parents, that the war had been pointless and that they had been lied to. They told their friends. Their friends told other friends. The lie that wars are won by socialist armies fighting just causes had been one of the load-bearing lies of the regime. After Afghanistan it would not bear weight anymore.

The Funerals of an Empire

Brezhnev died on November 10, 1982. He had been visibly ill for years - slurred speech, vacant pauses, the shuffle of a man kept upright by a pharmacopoeia of sedatives and stimulants administered by a personal nurse. The state funeral was enormous. Soldiers in greatcoats lined Red Square. The coffin was carried on a gun carriage. Andropov, the KGB chief, walked behind it and became the new General Secretary.

Andropov was sixty-eight and already dying of kidney failure, though no one outside a small circle knew it. He spent fifteen months in office, much of it in a hospital bed in Kuntsevo, hooked to a dialysis machine. He tried to discipline the workforce - police raided cinemas and bathhouses in the middle of the working day to catch people who should have been at their desks - and he promoted a younger group of officials, among them a fifty-one-year-old agriculture secretary from Stavropol named Mikhail Gorbachev. Then in February 1984 he too was dead. The Politburo chose Konstantin Chernenko, who was seventy-two, emphysemic, and barely able to read a speech without gasping. He lasted thirteen months. He was buried in March 1985.

Three General Secretaries in two and a half years. Three funerals on Red Square in twenty-eight months. The same generals, the same diplomats, the same Politburo members standing in the same coats in the same cold, watching another coffin go by. Western correspondents began to joke that they no longer bothered to unpack their black ties.

The joke that traveled fastest inside the country was a different one. A man tries to push his way into Red Square for one of the funerals. A militiaman stops him. "Comrade, you have no pass." The man waves him off. "I have a season ticket."

What no one yet quite said aloud was that the state itself was being buried in installments. The men who had built the system, who had survived Stalin and run the Five-Year Plans and signed The state was being buried in installments, and the joke about the season ticket traveled fastest because it was true. After Brezhnev came Andropov, and after Andropov came Chernenko, and after Chernenko there were no more men of that generation left. The Politburo that gathered in March 1985 had run out of safe choices. The man they nominated was twenty years younger than most of them, and he believed, in a way none of them quite did anymore, that the system could be saved. What he would discover was that some things, once questioned, cannot be put back.

Chapter 18
Gorbachev and the Unraveling

Perestroika and Glasnost

On the morning of March 11, 1985, the Politburo gathered in a room that smelled of cigarettes and old men. Konstantin Chernenko had died the previous evening, the third General Secretary to die in office in twenty-eight months. Andrei Gromyko, the foreign minister who had served Stalin, rose to nominate Mikhail Gorbachev. He was fifty-four years old, the youngest man in the room by a generation.

The country he inherited looked, from the outside, like a superpower. It had more nuclear warheads than the United States, an army of five million, and a flag that flew over half of Europe. From the inside it looked different. The economy had not grown in any meaningful sense for a decade. Oil revenues, which had propped up Brezhnev's stagnation, were falling. Soviet troops were dying in Afghanistan in a war no one in Moscow could explain. Shops in provincial cities sold pickled cabbage and little else. The life expectancy of Russian men was shrinking, pulled down by vodka and despair.

Gorbachev was a believer. That was the thing about him that his later opponents, both Communist and liberal, never quite forgave. He had not come to bury Lenin. He had come to save him. The system, he told the Central Committee, was sound at its foundations. What it needed was acceleration, *uskorenie*, and then, when acceleration proved insufficient, restructuring, *perestroika*, and then, when restructuring proved blocked at every turn by the apparatus he was trying to reform, openness, *glasnost*, so that the people themselves might push.

The first measures were modest and largely disastrous. A campaign against alcohol shut down distilleries, ripped up vineyards in Georgia and Moldova, and produced long queues outside the few shops still permitted to sell vodka. State revenue collapsed because the state had been making a great deal of money on drink. Sugar disappeared from shelves because people were using it to brew samogon at home. Within two years the campaign was quietly abandoned.

Alexander Yakovlev, who had spent ten years as ambassador to Canada watching how a different kind of society worked, was the intellectual at Gorbachev's elbow. He understood what his boss only partly admitted to himself: that you could not loosen one bolt in the Soviet machine without loosening all of them. Glasnost began as a tactic, a way to expose corrupt local bosses and force them out. By 1987 it had become something else. Newspapers began printing things that had been unsayable for sixty years. *Ogonyok*, a glossy weekly nobody had read, became the most dangerous magazine in the country. Films pulled from the shelves were screened. Solzhenitsyn was discussed in print. Bukharin was rehabilitated. Then Trotsky. Then, more cautiously, the question of Stalin himself.

For ordinary Soviet citizens the experience was vertiginous. A woman in Leningrad later remembered reading, in 1988, an account of the famine of 1932 in a journal her husband brought home from work. She had grown up in Ukraine. Her grandmother had died in that famine. For fifty-six years no one had been permitted to say the word. Now it was on her kitchen table in black and white. She read the article three times and then went and stood at the window for a long time without speaking.

Perestroika in the economy was harder. The Law on State Enterprise of 1987 gave factory managers more autonomy but kept the planning ministries intact, so that the managers now had two masters and obeyed neither. Cooperatives were permitted, the first legal private businesses since the 1920s. A few became wildly profitable. Most struggled. Shortages, which had been chronic, became acute. By 1989 sugar, soap, and cigarettes were rationed in Moscow. The queues lengthened. The newspapers, now free to report on the queues, made them feel longer still.

Gorbachev had wanted to reform a system. He was, without quite realizing it, dismantling one.

Chernobyl: The Wound That Could Not Be Hidden

At 1:23 in the morning on April 26, 1986, an operator at the Chernobyl nuclear power station in northern Ukraine pressed a button to initiate what was meant to be a safety test. Reactor No. 4 went critical, blew the thousand-ton concrete lid off its containment, and sent a plume of radioactive material into the night sky over the Pripyat marshes.

The first instinct of the system was the instinct it had always had: deny, delay, and contain the news rather than the contamination. Local officials in Pripyat let children go to school the next morning. A wedding party walked through the streets of the town while caesium-137 settled in the dust on their shoes. Moscow was not formally notified of the scale of the accident for hours. The world learned about it not from a Soviet announcement but from Swedish technicians at the Forsmark plant, eleven hundred kilometers away, whose radiation monitors had begun screaming when a worker came in from outside with contaminated boots.

For eighteen days Gorbachev said nothing in public. When he finally spoke on television, he was visibly angry, though more at the foreign press for what he called sensationalism than at the system that had hidden the truth from him. Behind the scenes he was furious for a different reason. He had been lied to. The bureaucracy that surrounded him, the ministries he was meant to lead, had told him for days that the situation was under control when it was not. He understood, perhaps for the first time, the depth of the rot.

Chernobyl killed thirty-one people directly in its first months. The longer count of cancers and shortened lives would run into the thousands and is still disputed. But the political wound was deeper than the medical one. The accident did to glasnost what no editorial could have done: it made openness a matter of survival. If a government could not tell its citizens that a reactor had exploded a hundred kilometers upwind, what else was it hiding? What had it always been hiding?

In Kyiv the May Day parade went ahead as planned, while officials in Moscow knew the wind was shifting south. Children marched past the reviewing stand under a sky that looked normal. The footage from that parade, when it was finally shown years later, would do more damage to Soviet authority in Ukraine than any dissident pamphlet. Ukrainian nationalism, dormant for decades, found its first mass grievance in the silence after the explosion.

Gorbachev himself later wrote that Chernobyl, more than any other single event, persuaded him that the old way could not continue. He was not the only one. Engineers, scientists, and journalists who had spent careers accepting the rules of what could and could not be said began testing the limits. A correspondent for *Pravda* wrote about safety violations at other Soviet reactors and was not fired. A physicist gave a press conference at which he criticized the design of the RBMK reactor that had failed. In the past he would have lost his job within a week. In 1986 he kept it.

The cloud from Chernobyl drifted across Belarus, Poland, Scandinavia, and eventually, in attenuated form, around the world. The political cloud drifted the other way, settling on Moscow, where it would not lift.

The Revolutions of 1989

The Brezhnev Doctrine had held, since 1968, that socialism in Eastern Europe was irreversible and that the Soviet Union would intervene with tanks if anyone tried to reverse it. Gorbachev quietly buried it. He told the Polish leader Wojciech Jaruzelski, and the Hungarian János Kádár, and anyone else who would listen, that their countries were their own problems. The Soviet army would not roll. He may not have grasped what this meant. Or perhaps he did, and accepted it.

In Poland the round-table talks between the Communist government and Solidarity opened in February 1989. By June, Solidarity had won every seat it was permitted to contest in semi-free elections. By August, Poland had a non-Communist prime minister. The Hungarian government opened its border with Austria in May, cutting the first hole in the Iron Curtain. East Germans on summer holidays in Hungary began, in small numbers and then in larger ones, simply walking west.

By autumn the trickle was a flood. East Germans crowded into the West German embassy in Prague and refused to leave. Erich Honecker, the East German leader, wanted to use force. Gorbachev, visiting East Berlin on October 7 for the fortieth anniversary of the German Democratic Republic, made it clear in private and almost in public that Soviet troops would stay in their barracks. *Wer zu spät kommt, den bestraft das Leben,* he is reported to have said. He who comes too late is punished by life. Honecker fell within two weeks.

On the evening of November 9, a confused East German spokesman named Günter Schabowski misread a note at a press conference and announced that new travel rules took effect immediately. Crowds went to the Wall. The guards, who had received no orders, opened the gates. By morning people were dancing on the concrete and selling pieces of it as souvenirs.

The pace was bewildering. Czechoslovakia's Velvet Revolution unseated its government in eleven days. Bulgaria's leader was pushed out by his own Politburo. Romania, alone, turned violent: Nicolae Ceaușescu and his wife were tried in a school gymnasium on Christmas Day and shot against a wall in the courtyard outside. The footage was broadcast within hours.

In Moscow the response was a strange mixture of pride and panic. Gorbachev had ended the Cold War. He had earned, and in 1990 received, the Nobel Peace Prize. Western leaders adored him. Inside the Soviet Union his standing collapsed. The hardliners in the army and the KGB watched the outer empire disappear in three months and asked themselves how long the inner empire could last. The reformers asked themselves whether the man at the top could keep up with what he had started.

The Baltic republics provided the answer first. Lithuania declared independence in March 1990. Estonia and Latvia followed. In January 1991 Soviet special forces stormed the television tower in Vilnius, killing fourteen people. Gorbachev claimed afterward to have known nothing in advance. Whether that was true or not, it satisfied no one. The hardliners thought he had wavered; the democrats thought he had given the order. In Russia itself, Boris Yeltsin, who had been expelled from the Politburo in 1987 and had rebuilt his career as a populist tribune, was elected chairman of the Russian Supreme Soviet, and then, in June 1991, the first popularly elected leader in a thousand years of Russian history. There were now two presidents in the Kremlin, one of a union that was coming apart, one of its largest republic. They did not like each other.

The August Coup

Gorbachev spent the first part of August 1991 at his dacha at Foros, on the Crimean coast, working on the text of a new Union treaty. The treaty was meant to save what could be saved: a looser federation in which the republics would have real sovereignty and Moscow would retain only what they freely ceded. The March referendum had shown that 76 percent of voters wanted to preserve the union in some form. The signing ceremony was scheduled for August 20.

On the afternoon of August 18, a delegation of senior officials arrived at Foros uninvited. They had cut the telephone lines on the way in. They told Gorbachev that a state of emergency was about to be declared and asked him to sign the decree or transfer his powers to Vice President Gennady Yanayev. He refused. They placed him under house arrest.

The men behind the coup were the men Gorbachev had appointed to his own inner circle: Vladimir Kryuchkov, the head of the KGB; Dmitry Yazov, the defense minister; Boris Pugo, the interior minister; Valentin Pavlov, the prime minister. They believed they were saving the country. They had read the draft Union treaty and concluded that it amounted to the dissolution of the Soviet state. In a sense they were right. In every other sense their plan was a catastrophe.

It began with a press conference on the morning of August 19. Yanayev sat in front of the cameras with his hands visibly shaking. He announced that Gorbachev was ill and that an Emergency Committee had assumed power. Tanks rolled into Moscow. Tchaikovsky's *Swan Lake* played on every television channel, with bulletins between the acts.

Boris Yeltsin was at his own dacha when the news came through. He drove to the Russian White House, the parliament building of the Russian Federation, on the embankment of the Moskva River. By midday a crowd had begun to gather around it; by afternoon there were thousands. Yeltsin walked out, climbed onto a tank of the Taman Division that had been ordered to surround the building, and read a statement denouncing the coup as illegal. A photographer caught the image. It traveled around the world before the conspirators in the Kremlin had decided what to do next.

They had decided very little. They had not arrested Yeltsin, though they had the opportunity. They had not cut the city's communications, so foreign journalists filed copy freely and Russian citizens with fax machines and the new mobile telephones spread word of the resistance. They had not secured the army's loyalty beyond the unit commanders. When the order came to storm the White House on the night of August 20, two of the three generals tasked with the operation refused. Soldiers in the tanks around the building turned their turrets away in a gesture that was understood by everyone watching.

Three young men died that night in a tunnel near the Garden Ring, crushed under an armored personnel carrier in a confused scuffle. They were the only fatalities of the coup. By the morning of August 21, Kryuchkov and Yazov were on a plane to Foros, hoping to make peace with the president they had imprisoned. Gorbachev refused to see them. Pugo shot himself. The marshal Sergei Akhromeyev, who had supported the plotters, hanged himself in his Kremlin office.

Gorbachev flew back to Moscow on the night of August 22. He stepped off the plane in a sweater, looking exhausted, and gave a press conference in which he insisted that the Communist Party could still be reformed. He had not yet understood. The country he returned to was not the country he had left four days earlier. Yeltsin had stood on a tank. Gorbachev had been a prisoner. Power had shifted, and there was no shifting it back.

*In August 1991, hardline Communist plotters sent armored columns
into Moscow to reverse Gorbachev's reforms-only to find their
authority dissolve against crowds of citizens and a defiant Boris Yeltsin
standing on a tank.*

The Soviet Union Dissolves

The first thing Yeltsin did, when Gorbachev appeared before the
Russian parliament on August 23, was to humiliate him. With
cameras rolling he made the Soviet president read aloud the
minutes of a cabinet meeting in which Gorbachev's own ministers
had supported the coup. Then Yeltsin signed, in front of him, a
decree suspending the activities of the Communist Party on
Russian territory. Gorbachev stood at the podium with the paper in
his hand and did not know what to say.

The republics did not wait. Ukraine declared independence on
August 24. Belarus the following day. Moldova, Azerbaijan,
Uzbekistan, Kyrgyzstan, Tajikistan, Armenia, Turkmenistan, all in
the next weeks. The Baltic states, whose independence Moscow
had refused to recognize, were recognized now by the United
States, by the European Community, and finally, on September 6,

by what remained of the Soviet government itself.

Gorbachev kept trying. Through September and October he convened meetings, drafted new versions of the Union treaty, telephoned republican presidents who increasingly did not return his calls. The decisive vote came on December 1, when Ukrainians went to the polls and 92 percent of them, including a majority in every region, including Crimea, voted for independence. Without Ukraine there could be no union. Yeltsin understood this immediately.

On December 8, in a hunting lodge in the Belovezha Forest in Belarus, Yeltsin met with the Ukrainian president Leonid Kravchuk and the Belarusian chairman Stanislav Shushkevich. They signed a document declaring that the Soviet Union, as a subject of international law and a geopolitical reality, had ceased to exist. They telephoned the American president George Bush before they telephoned Gorbachev. When Gorbachev was finally told, he was furious, and powerless. He had been the head of a state that three men in a forest had abolished over breakfast.

On December 21, in Alma-Ata, eleven of the twelve remaining republics formalized the dissolution and announced the Commonwealth of Independent States. Georgia, then in the throes of its own civil war, did not attend. The Soviet Union had four days left.

On the evening of December 25, 1991, Gorbachev sat at a desk in the Kremlin and read a short resignation speech to a television camera. He spoke of his pride in what had been accomplished, of his regrets, of his hope. He signed the decree transferring control of the nuclear arsenal to Yeltsin. The pen did not work. An American television producer in the room handed him another one.

At 7:32 in the evening, the red flag with the hammer and sickle was lowered from the dome of the Senate building. It was folded by a soldier who had been told to be careful. The white, blue, and red tricolor of the Russian Federation was raised in its place. The temperature in Moscow was minus four degrees. Snow had been falling on and off all day. In the square below, almost no one had gathered to watch.

The flag came down at 7:32 in the evening and the soldier folded it carefully. In the square below, almost no one had gathered to watch. The state that had been buried in installments had finally been buried whole, and what came next was not a plan but an improvisation, carried out by a man who had climbed onto a tank in August and now stood, six months later, at the head of a country whose institutions, currency, and economic logic had all dissolved together. The 1990s would be lived as a long emergency by people who had been promised, briefly, something else.

Chapter 19
Wild Capitalism: The Yeltsin Years

Shock Therapy and the Great Sell-Off

On January 2, 1992, Russians woke up to a country where prices were free. Bread that had cost a few kopecks the day before now cost what the seller asked. Milk, sausage, soap, vodka, shoes - everything that had moved through the Soviet system at fixed prices was suddenly attached to a number that climbed by the hour. By the end of the year, prices had risen roughly 2,500 percent. The savings of a lifetime, kept in passbook accounts at Sberbank, evaporated. Pensioners who had put away rubles for forty years discovered that what they had was no longer enough to buy a winter coat.

This was shock therapy. The young economists around Yeltsin - Yegor Gaidar most prominent among them, with Anatoly Chubais running the privatization side - believed the Soviet command economy could not be reformed gradually. It had to be broken open all at once and exposed to the air. Half-measures, in their view, had killed Gorbachev's perestroika. The model came from Poland, where a similar program under Leszek Balcerowicz had produced a sharp recession followed by recovery. Western advisors, including the American economist Jeffrey Sachs, urged Yeltsin to move fast. The International Monetary Fund agreed.

The recession came. The recovery did not. Russian industry, built for a planned economy and an empire that no longer existed, could not survive contact with world prices. Factories that had employed whole towns shut down or kept the lights on by paying workers in the goods they produced - bricks, pots, light bulbs - which workers then tried to sell by the roadside. Salaries went unpaid for months. Doctors, teachers, engineers, soldiers: all of them learned to wait.

Then came privatization. In 1992 and 1993, every Russian citizen received a voucher worth ten thousand rubles, meant to represent their share of the national wealth. In theory, ordinary people would become shareholders in the enterprises where they worked. In practice, most Russians sold their vouchers immediately - for cash, for a bottle of vodka, for whatever they could get - because they needed to eat. The vouchers were bought up cheap by anyone with the capital and connections to do so. Whole oil fields, nickel mines, and metallurgical combines changed hands at fractions of their value.

The second wave was worse. By 1995 the government was broke and faced a presidential election the following year against a resurgent Communist Party. Chubais and a group of well-placed bankers proposed a deal that came to be called loans-for-shares. The bankers would lend the state money. As collateral, they would receive controlling stakes in the country's most valuable companies - Yukos, Lukoil, Norilsk Nickel, Sibneft. When the state inevitably failed to repay the loans, the bankers would keep the shares. The auctions were rigged. The winners were almost always the same people who had organized the scheme. In a matter of months, a handful of men acquired industrial assets worth tens of billions of dollars for a fraction of their value.

These were the oligarchs. Boris Berezovsky, who had moved from selling cars to controlling oil. Mikhail Khodorkovsky, a former Komsomol activist who now ran Yukos. Vladimir Gusinsky, who built a media empire. Vladimir Potanin, the architect of the loans-for-shares scheme itself, who emerged with Norilsk Nickel. Roman Abramovich, younger and quieter, gathering pieces of the oil industry. They were not, in any ordinary sense, capitalists. They were men who had been close enough to power at the right moment.

The cost to ordinary Russians is hard to overstate. Life expectancy for men fell from sixty-four in 1990 to fifty-seven by 1994. Alcoholism, suicide, and heart disease spiked. The country lost more people to despair than it had to many of its smaller wars. In Moscow, a class of newly rich men in leather jackets drove imported cars past lines of pensioners selling their possessions on the pavement. The Soviet world had not so much ended as turned inside out.

The Constitutional Crisis of 1993

Yeltsin had inherited a parliament elected under Soviet rules in 1990, when the Communist Party still ran everything and nobody had imagined the country would fall apart within eighteen months. The Congress of People's Deputies and its standing body, the Supreme Soviet, were stuffed with men who had owed their seats to the old system. By 1992 they were furious about shock therapy, about the collapse of the ruble, about the humiliation of seeing a superpower reduced to begging Western banks for credits.

The leader of the opposition inside the building was Yeltsin's own vice president, Alexander Rutskoy, a decorated Afghan war pilot with a thick mustache and a taste for blunt speech. Alongside him stood Ruslan Khasbulatov, the speaker of the parliament, a Chechen academic with a sharper political mind than Rutskoy and a deeper grudge. Through 1992 and into 1993 the two sides traded accusations and decrees. Yeltsin called for emergency powers. The Congress voted to strip them away. A referendum in April 1993 gave the president a slim mandate to continue, but resolved nothing.

On September 21, 1993, Yeltsin signed Decree 1400. It dissolved the Congress and the Supreme Soviet and called for elections to a new legislature in December. The decree was, by the existing constitution, illegal. The Constitutional Court said so. The parliament met in emergency session and voted to impeach Yeltsin, swearing Rutskoy in as acting president. For ten days Russia had two governments, one in the Kremlin and one barricaded inside the White House - the same white marble building where Yeltsin himself had stood on a tank two years earlier defying the August coup.

The siege tightened. Yeltsin cut off electricity and telephone lines to the parliament. Crowds of supporters gathered around the building. On October 3, the situation broke. Armed supporters of Rutskoy and Khasbulatov pushed past police lines, seized the mayor's office across the street, and set off toward the Ostankino television tower. Rutskoy, standing on a balcony, urged them on. A firefight at Ostankino killed dozens. Yeltsin declared a state of emergency.

The army hesitated. Senior commanders were reluctant to take sides in what looked like a quarrel among politicians, and several units refused orders before the defense minister, Pavel Grachev, was finally given a written directive he could act on. Just after dawn on October 4, tanks rolled onto the bridge facing the White House and opened fire. Russians and foreign correspondents watched on television as shells punched into the upper floors of the parliament building and black smoke poured from the windows. By the afternoon the building had been stormed. Rutskoy and Khasbulatov were marched out and taken to Lefortovo prison. The official death toll for the two days reached 147; the real number was probably higher.

Yeltsin had won. In December his new constitution was put to a referendum and approved, although turnout figures were disputed almost from the day they were released. The constitution gave the president sweeping powers: he appointed the prime minister, could dissolve the lower house, and ruled by decree on a wide range of matters. The new parliament, the State Duma, was weaker than the body it replaced. Russian democracy now had a framework, and the framework had a strong man at its center.

The same building Yeltsin had defended in 1991 he had shelled in 1993. People noticed.

The First Chechen War

Chechnya had declared independence in 1991, under a former Soviet air force general named Dzhokhar Dudayev. For three years Moscow ignored the problem and hoped it would solve itself. It did not. By 1994 Dudayev's republic in the northern Caucasus was a country in everything but international recognition, with its own flag, its own currency arrangements, and a thriving traffic in oil, weapons, and counterfeit rubles that embarrassed the federal government every week.

In December 1994, Yeltsin ordered the army in. His defense minister, Pavel Grachev - the same Grachev who had ordered the tanks against the White House the previous October - boasted that he could take Grozny, the Chechen capital, in two hours with a single airborne regiment. The boast became one of the cruelest jokes of the decade.

The Russian column that rolled toward Grozny on New Year's Eve was made up of conscripts, many of them teenagers, some of whom had been given the keys to a tank a few weeks before. They drove into the city center without proper maps, without coordinated infantry support, and without any clear sense of where the enemy was. The Chechens, fighting on streets they knew, used rocket-propelled grenades from upper windows and basements to immobilize the lead and rear vehicles of each column, then destroyed everything trapped in between. The Maikop Brigade lost most of its men and nearly all its armor in a few hours around the railway station. Russian bodies lay frozen in the snow for weeks.

The army adjusted by doing what the Soviet army had always done: bringing up artillery and reducing the city block by block. By February 1995, Grozny had been pounded into rubble that resembled photographs of Berlin in 1945. The Chechens withdrew into the mountains and fought a guerrilla war that the Russian army, demoralized and underfunded, was not equipped to win.

What made the war unlike any previous Russian conflict was television. Reporters from NTV, the new private channel owned by

Gusinsky, traveled with Russian units and Chechen fighters alike. Russians at home watched their own conscripts dying in real time, on the evening news, in color. Mothers organized to find their sons. Coffins came back to towns from the Urals to the Pacific. Public support for the war, never strong, collapsed.

In June 1995, a Chechen field commander named Shamil Basayev led a raid into the southern Russian town of Budyonnovsk, seized a hospital, and took more than a thousand hostages. Russian special forces botched two rescue attempts. In the end the prime minister, Viktor Chernomyrdin, negotiated with Basayev directly on live television - a humiliation broadcast into every home in the country - and the hostage-takers were allowed to drive back to Chechnya. A year later, in August 1996, Chechen fighters retook Grozny in a stunning operation that caught the Russian garrison entirely by surprise.

That was enough. Yeltsin, freshly reelected and visibly ill, sent his security chief Alexander Lebed to negotiate. The Khasavyurt Accord, signed in August 1996, ended the fighting and deferred the question of Chechnya's status by five years. By any honest reckoning, Russia had lost. Estimates of the dead ranged from 30,000 to 100,000, most of them Chechen civilians. A generation of Russian officers came out of the war convinced that they had been betrayed by politicians, by journalists, and by the country at large. They would remember.

Oligarchs, Bandits, and the 1998 Default

By the mid-1990s the line between business and crime in Russia had become a matter of definition. Every café, every kiosk, every restaurant paid protection money to somebody - a local gang, a sports club turned racketeer, a private security firm staffed by former KGB officers, or some combination of all three. Contract killings in Moscow ran into the hundreds each year. Bankers were shot getting out of their cars. Journalists who wrote about the wrong oligarch were beaten in stairwells. The American magazine *Forbes*, in a 1996 cover story, called Berezovsky the godfather of the Kremlin; Berezovsky sued, but the article captured something true about how power worked.

The oligarchs who had emerged from loans-for-shares now controlled most of the country's exportable wealth and a great deal of its media. Berezovsky owned ORT, the main state television channel, in everything but name. Gusinsky owned NTV. Their channels savaged each other and savaged anyone the proprietors wished savaged. In 1996, faced with a Communist candidate, Gennady Zyuganov, who was leading in the polls, the oligarchs put their resources behind Yeltsin and ran a campaign of fear, money, and saturation coverage that pulled him over the finish line. Yeltsin disappeared between rounds with what was later admitted to be a serious heart attack. His advisors hid his condition and won the election anyway.

The economy, meanwhile, was running on borrowed time and borrowed money. The government covered its deficits by issuing short-term ruble-denominated bonds called GKOs, paying interest rates that climbed past 100 percent annually. Foreign investors, drawn by the yields, poured money in. Russian banks borrowed in dollars to buy GKOs in rubles. The whole structure depended on the ruble staying stable against the dollar and on the price of oil holding up.

In the summer of 1998 both assumptions failed. The Asian financial crisis of 1997 had already shaken emerging markets. Oil prices fell below ten dollars a barrel. Tax collection inside Russia was a fiction. On August 17, 1998, the government devalued the ruble, defaulted on its domestic debt, and froze payments to foreign creditors. The ruble lost three-quarters of its value within weeks. Banks closed their doors with customers' deposits inside. A second wave of small savers lost what they had managed to accumulate since 1992.

The political effects were as serious as the economic ones. Yeltsin fired his prime minister and tried to bring back Chernomyrdin; the Duma refused. He settled on Yevgeny Primakov, a former foreign minister and intelligence chief, who steadied the situation but represented a kind of Soviet-era continuity that Yeltsin's inner circle - now openly called the Family, and including his daughter Tatyana and Berezovsky - found threatening. Primakov was dismissed in May 1999, as was his successor, Sergei Stepashin, three months later. The country was running through prime ministers like ammunition.

What 1998 broke was not only the economy but the idea that the 1990s had been a transition to something better. Inflation, defaults, the wars, the killings, the spectacle of a few men buying yachts while pensioners sold their shoes - it added up to a verdict on the decade that Russians delivered in opinion polls year after year. Whatever they had wanted in 1991, this was not it.

Yeltsin's Choice

In August 1999, Yeltsin appointed his fifth prime minister in seventeen months. The man was almost unknown: a former KGB lieutenant colonel who had run the FSB, the domestic successor agency, for the previous year. His name was Vladimir Putin. He was forty-six, slight, soft-spoken, with cold blue eyes and a habit of arriving early to meetings.

Within weeks of Putin's appointment, apartment buildings in Moscow, Buinaksk, and Volgodonsk were destroyed by bombs in the night. Nearly three hundred people died. The government blamed Chechen terrorists. A device discovered in a basement in Ryazan, which FSB officers later claimed was a training exercise, raised questions that have never been fully resolved; historians differ on what happened in Ryazan and on the broader question of responsibility for the bombings. What is not in dispute is the political effect. Russians, terrified, demanded action. Putin promised it in language that nobody who heard it would forget, vowing to hunt down the terrorists wherever they were found, even in the outhouse. He sent the army back into Chechnya. The second war was different from the first: better prepared, more brutal, and overwhelmingly popular at home.

Putin's approval ratings climbed from single digits in August to over 50 percent by November. The pro-Kremlin party hastily assembled to fight the December Duma elections, Unity, did well enough to break the opposition's grip on the lower house. The Family had found what it needed: a successor who could win, who looked like a man in control, and who - they believed - would protect them from prosecution after Yeltsin left office.

On the morning of December 31, 1999, Yeltsin recorded a televised address. He sat at his desk in a dark suit, his face puffy and his voice thick, and he asked Russians to forgive him. He had believed, he said, that he could carry the country across in one leap from the gray, stagnant, totalitarian past to a bright, prosperous, civilized future. It had not worked out that way. The leap had been too hard. Many of the hopes had not come true. He was resigning. Russia would enter the new millennium with a new president.

That afternoon Putin signed his first decree as acting president. It granted Yeltsin and his family lifetime immunity from criminal prosecution.

Outside, in Moscow, it was snowing. Fireworks went off at midnight as they did every year. In the apartments along the ring road, people raised glasses to the new century and watched, on television, a younger man they barely knew step forward to take the oath.

The fireworks went off at midnight and the apartments along the ring road raised glasses to a new century and a younger man they barely knew. Yeltsin had asked forgiveness for the dreams that had not come true. His successor would make no such apologies. The lifetime immunity granted that afternoon was the first signal of how the next transition would work, and of who would benefit. The man taking the oath had spent his career in the shadows of the security services, and he had ideas about Russia that the cameras at midnight had not yet had occasion to record.

Chapter 20
The Rise of Vladimir Putin

From Petersburg to the Kremlin

On the last night of the twentieth century, while most Russians were pouring vodka and watching fireworks crackle over the Kremlin walls, Boris Yeltsin sat in front of a television camera and resigned. He was tired, and he looked it. His face was puffy, his speech slow, his sentences heavy with the apologies of a man who had run out of room. He asked forgiveness for the dreams that had not come true. Then he handed the country to a man almost no one in it could yet picture clearly.

Vladimir Vladimirovich Putin was forty-seven years old. He had been prime minister for five months. Before that he had run the FSB, the domestic successor to the KGB. Before that he had been a deputy mayor in St. Petersburg, working for the liberal Anatoly Sobchak through the rough years when the city was renamed and its old certainties dismantled. And before that, for most of his adult life, he had been a mid-ranking officer in Soviet intelligence, posted to Dresden, watching from a window as the East German state dissolved around him and Moscow refused to answer the phone.

That last detail mattered. Putin had told the story himself, more than once: the crowds outside the Stasi building, the documents being burned in a furnace until the furnace gave out, the call to a Red Army command center that produced only silence. Moscow, he said, was silent. The silence had stayed with him.

He had come to the Kremlin late and almost by accident. In 1996 he moved to Moscow to take a job in the presidential property department, the kind of post that rewards loyalty and rewards it discreetly. He rose quickly. By 1998 he was head of the FSB. By

August 1999 he was prime minister, the fifth in less than two years, and most observers assumed he would last as long as the others, which was not long. Yeltsin's circle, the so-called Family, was looking for a successor who could protect them after Yeltsin left. They needed someone competent, someone loyal, someone who would not put them in prison or send them into exile. Putin fit. He was disciplined, he did not drink to excess, he did not give interviews he had not thought through. He had spent his career taking orders and keeping confidences. What no one in the Family quite saw, in those late summer weeks of 1999, was that they had chosen a man who would outlast all of them.

The country he inherited on New Year's Eve was bruised. The ruble had collapsed in 1998, wiping out the savings of millions. Wages went unpaid for months at a time; teachers and miners struck and were ignored. In the regions, governors ran their territories as private fiefdoms, signing trade deals with foreign companies and ignoring federal tax demands. A handful of men, the oligarchs, had taken ownership of the country's oil, nickel, aluminum, and television networks during the privatizations of the mid-1990s, and they wore their wealth openly. Public opinion polls in 1999 found that ordinary Russians thought of the previous decade as a humiliation. They wanted order. They wanted to be paid. They wanted to stop being embarrassed by their own state.

Putin, on the day he became acting president, signed a decree guaranteeing Yeltsin and his family immunity from prosecution. Then he flew to Chechnya to spend New Year's with Russian troops.

The Second Chechen War

The war had already begun. In August and September 1999, a series of apartment buildings in Moscow, Buinaksk, and Volgodonsk exploded in the middle of the night, killing more than three hundred people in their beds. The bombings were blamed on Chechen militants. A fourth device, found in the basement of a building in Ryazan, was defused; the FSB later said it had been a training exercise. The official account satisfied many Russians at the time. It has been contested ever since, by journalists and by some of those who later fell out with the Kremlin, and the question of who placed the bombs remains one of the most disputed in modern Russian history.

What is not in dispute is the political effect. By the autumn of 1999, Russian troops were moving into Chechnya for the second time in five years, and the country was rallying behind the new prime minister. The first Chechen war, fought between 1994 and 1996, had been a disaster: a humiliating ceasefire, Russian conscripts dying in Grozny apartment blocks, generals contradicting one another on television. Yeltsin had been broken by it. Putin promised a different kind of war.

"We will pursue the terrorists everywhere," he said in September 1999, in a phrase that became famous. "If we catch them in the toilet, we will wipe them out in the outhouse." The language was crude, deliberately so. It came from the slang of the streets and the army barracks, and it announced a tone that had been missing from the Kremlin for years.

The second war was fought differently from the first. Artillery was used freely, including in cities. Grozny, the Chechen capital, was bombarded for months and reduced, by early 2000, to something the United Nations would later call the most destroyed city on earth. Civilian casualties were heavy and largely uncounted. Filtration camps were set up to screen Chechen men of fighting age. Independent journalists who tried to report from the field, the most prominent being Anna Politkovskaya, found themselves harassed, detained, and eventually, in her case, killed.

For most Russians, the war was distant and the news from it was controlled. What they saw was a prime minister who flew to military bases, who spoke in short sentences, who handed out hunting knives to pilots. His approval rating, which had been around two percent when he took office in August, climbed past fifty by November. In March 2000 he was elected president in the first round.

Victory in Chechnya, when it came, was political rather than military. By 2003 Putin had found a Chechen who would govern the republic on Moscow's behalf: Akhmad Kadyrov, a former mufti who had fought against Russia in the first war and then changed sides. Kadyrov was given a free hand, federal money, and personal control of a security force drawn from former rebels. In May 2004 he was killed by a bomb planted under the reviewing stand at a Victory Day parade in Grozny. His son Ramzan, then twenty-seven, inherited the republic in time.

Four months after the elder Kadyrov's death, in September 2004, a group of armed men seized a school in the North Ossetian town of Beslan on the first day of the academic year. They held more than a thousand hostages, most of them children, in a gymnasium wired with explosives. After three days the building was stormed. More than three hundred people died, half of them children. Putin, addressing the country afterward, did not dwell on the failures of the security services. He spoke instead of weakness, of an attack on Russia itself, and of the changes that would now be required to make the country strong.

The Vertical of Power

The phrase Putin used, over and over in those early years, was the vertical of power. *Vertikal vlasti.* He meant a chain of command that ran from the Kremlin down to the smallest district administration without breaks or detours. The Russia he had inherited was horizontal: governors negotiated with Moscow, oligarchs negotiated with governors, television networks owned by oligarchs negotiated with everyone. Putin set out to make all of it vertical, and he was patient about it.

The oligarchs went first. In the summer of 2000, a few months into his presidency, Putin called the country's leading businessmen to a meeting at a state dacha outside Moscow. The terms he offered them were never written down, but everyone present understood. They could keep what they had taken in the 1990s. They would pay their taxes. They would stay out of politics. If they crossed any of these lines, the state would come for them, and the state, under its new management, would win.

Two of them tested the proposition early. Vladimir Gusinsky, who owned the NTV television network and whose journalists had mocked Putin during the 1999 campaign, was arrested in June 2000 on fraud charges, held for three days, and released only after signing over his media holdings. He left the country. Boris Berezovsky, the kingmaker of the late Yeltsin years, the man who had arguably done more than anyone to put Putin in the Kremlin, fell out with him over coverage of the sinking of the submarine Kursk in August 2000. Berezovsky lost his television station and then his country; he died in exile in England in 2013, in circumstances his friends never accepted as suicide.

The third example was the one that made the rules unmistakable. Mikhail Khodorkovsky, owner of the oil company Yukos and at one point the richest man in Russia, had begun funding opposition parties and speaking openly about corruption at the top of the government. In October 2003 his private plane was stopped on a runway in Siberia and he was arrested at gunpoint by masked agents. He was tried, convicted of fraud and tax evasion, and sent to a prison colony east of Lake Baikal. Yukos was broken up; most of its assets ended up in the hands of the state oil company Rosneft. Khodorkovsky spent ten years in prison. The other oligarchs took the lesson.

The governors came next. After Beslan, Putin announced that regional governors would no longer be elected by their populations but appointed by the president and confirmed by regional legislatures. The change was presented as a security measure. Its effect was to end, in a single stroke, one of the few federal features of the post-Soviet constitution. Governors who had built independent power bases became, overnight, employees of the Kremlin.

Then the media. By the end of Putin's first term, every major national television channel was either owned by the state or by companies close to it. Newspapers and websites still operated more freely, especially in Moscow, and a small independent press continued to do serious work. But for the seventy or eighty percent of Russians who got their news from television, the picture had become uniform. The president was shown flying jets, swimming in Siberian rivers, riding horses bare-chested, descending in a submersible to inspect the wreck of a Greek freighter. He was shown listening, gravely, to the complaints of pensioners. He was not shown being criticized.

Inside the government, the men Putin trusted were the ones he had known the longest. Many came from his St. Petersburg years; many came from the security services. The press began to call them the *siloviki*, from the Russian word for force. They moved into the boards of state companies, into the ministries, into the presidential administration. They did not have to be brilliant. They had to be loyal, and they had to understand that loyalty was the currency of the system.

By 2005 the vertical was largely built. The federal government collected its taxes. The governors took their orders. The oligarchs paid their dues. The television was friendly. What remained was to give the system a name that sounded democratic, and to keep the money flowing.

Petrostate Prosperity

In 1998, the price of a barrel of Brent crude oil fell below ten dollars. In 2008, it reached one hundred and forty. The arc of those ten years was, in a sense, the arc of Putin's first two terms. He had taken office at the bottom of the oil market and presided over a climb that no Russian leader had ever enjoyed.

Russia in 2000 was, and still is, one of the world's largest producers of oil and natural gas. When prices were low, this was a curse: the budget could not be balanced, the ruble could not be defended, the regions could not be paid. When prices rose, everything changed. Tax revenues poured into Moscow. Wages were paid on time, then raised. Pensions came regularly. The state paid off the foreign debts that Yeltsin had begged the IMF to reschedule. A stabilization fund was created to absorb the surplus and a sovereign wealth fund grew alongside it.

For ordinary Russians, the change was felt in small, daily ways. Salaries that had been delayed for months arrived on the first of the month. Cars filled the streets of Moscow and then of the regional capitals. Apartments long owned in name but never refurbished were renovated. Foreign holidays, once the preserve of the very rich, became possible for office workers from Yekaterinburg or Novosibirsk. Mortgage lending appeared. So did consumer credit. So, eventually, did IKEA, on the outskirts of every large city.

The Russian economy grew, in real terms, by an average of around seven percent a year between 1999 and 2008. Real disposable income roughly doubled. Poverty, as the government measured it, fell by more than half. None of this was distributed evenly. Moscow boomed while villages in the Russian north emptied out. A new class of very rich Russians appeared, buying football clubs in London and ski chalets in Courchevel, and the gap between them and a pensioner in Voronezh became wider than anything that had existed under the Soviets. Corruption, by every available measure, worsened. State contracts were a route to private wealth, and the route was well trodden.

But for most of his first two terms, the broad trend pointed up, and Putin received the credit. Whether he had caused the boom or merely been lucky in the price of oil was a question argued in academic journals and rarely on Russian television. To the public, the link was simple. Under Yeltsin, the shelves had been full but no one had money. Under Putin, the money had come back.

The pride that returned with the prosperity was, for many Russians, the more important gain. Foreign reporters who travelled outside Moscow in those years often came back with the same set of quotations: people who said they did not need democracy in the abstract, they needed to feel they lived in a country that mattered. Putin, they said, had given them that. He had stopped apologizing to the West. He had reminded the world that Russia was a great power. The G8 met in St. Petersburg in 2006 and the city was scrubbed for the cameras. The Olympic Games were awarded to Sochi in 2007. Russia, it seemed, was being treated again the way Russians believed it deserved.

Managed Democracy

The phrase was coined by one of Putin's own advisers, Vladislav Surkov, the deputy head of the presidential administration who served as the system's chief political technologist for most of the first decade. Surkov preferred a slightly different formulation: sovereign democracy. The choice of words mattered to him. Russia, he argued, was a democracy. It held elections. It had a parliament, a constitution, courts, a free press in the formal sense. What it did not have, and would not have, was a politics imposed from outside or a politics that risked the country's coherence. Sovereignty came first. Democracy came in the form the country could bear.

In practice, the system worked like this. Elections were held on schedule. Multiple parties competed. Votes were counted, mostly, more or less. But the rules around the elections - the access to media, the registration of candidates, the funding of parties, the use of administrative resources by incumbents - were all calibrated so that the outcome was known in advance. The dominant party, United Russia, was assembled from the wreckage of earlier pro-Kremlin movements in 2001 and became, over the following years, the vehicle for almost every governor, mayor, and bureaucrat who wanted to keep his job. It did not have an ideology. It had Putin.

Opposition existed, but it was managed. The Communists remained as a kind of permanent runner-up, useful for the appearance of contest. The Liberal Democratic Party, led by the showman Vladimir Zhirinovsky, supplied flamboyant nationalism that drained off some of the energy that might otherwise have gone elsewhere. A new party, Just Russia, was created to absorb left-leaning voters who might have drifted to the Communists. Liberals of the 1990s, the heirs of the reformers, were squeezed out of the Duma in the 2003 elections and never returned in significant numbers.

The constitution limited a president to two consecutive terms. Putin's second term ended in 2008. He did not change the constitution, then. Instead he engineered the election of Dmitry Medvedev, his longtime aide, a quieter and smaller man whom Western observers initially hoped might be a liberal. Medvedev took the presidency. Putin became prime minister. The two governed together in what was called the tandem, and there was never serious doubt about who made the decisions. Four years later, in 2012, Putin returned to the Kremlin, this time for a term that had been extended, by an obliging amendment, from four years to six.

By then the system had a name and a logic that even its critics had to acknowledge worked, in its own terms. The Kremlin set the boundaries. Within those boundaries, life could be lived. Russians could travel, start businesses, buy property, criticize the local mayor in private, watch satellite television, read what they liked on the internet. What they could not do was organize against the center, build national political movements outside the approved ones, or run independent candidates with any real chance of winning. Those who tried discovered, one by one, the limits.

The journalist Anna Politkovskaya was shot in the elevator of her Moscow apartment building on the seventh of October 2006. It was Putin's fifty-fourth birthday. The killers were eventually convicted. The person who ordered the killing was never publicly identified. Her colleagues continued, for a while, to put out the newspaper she had written for, and her last unfinished article, on torture in Chechnya, was published with the columns left blank where her sentences had not yet been written.

The columns where Politkovskaya's sentences had not yet been written were left blank, and her colleagues continued for a while to put out the newspaper. The limits she had discovered were being mapped, one journalist and one opposition figure at a time, by the system that had grown up around the man who took the oath at midnight in 1999. What that system would do once it felt itself strong enough to act outside its own borders, and what it would do when it felt itself threatened from within them, was the question the next decade would answer.

Chapter 21
Empire's Return: Russia in the Twenty-First Century

Color Revolutions and the Fear of Contagion

On a cold November night in 2004, the square in central Kyiv filled with people in orange scarves who refused to go home. They had been told their vote did not count. The official result handed the presidency to Viktor Yanukovych, the candidate Moscow had backed, who had visited Vladimir Putin twice during the campaign and received his open endorsement. The protesters believed the count was a fraud. Within weeks, a rerun election was ordered, and Viktor Yushchenko, the candidate Moscow had not wanted, became president of Ukraine.

Putin watched this happen from the Kremlin, and he drew a lesson from it that would shape the next twenty years of Russian foreign policy.

The Orange Revolution did not happen in isolation. A year earlier, in Tbilisi, crowds carrying roses had walked into the Georgian parliament and persuaded Eduard Shevardnadze - the old Soviet foreign minister turned Georgian president - to resign. Four months after the Ukrainian rerun, demonstrators in Bishkek stormed the presidential offices and drove the Kyrgyz president from the country in what came to be called the Tulip Revolution. Behind all of them, in the Kremlin's reading, stood the example of Belgrade in 2000, when Serbian crowds had brought down Slobodan Milošević after a disputed election.

To the people in those squares, the revolutions were about stolen elections, oligarchic theft, police brutality, and the simple desire not to be lied to by their own governments. To Putin and the men around him, they were something else: a method. A pattern repeated across the former Soviet space could not be accidental. There had to be a hand behind it.

The hand, in their telling, was American. Sergei Lavrov, the foreign minister, spoke of color revolutions as a technology of regime change developed in Washington and exported wherever the United States wished to install a friendlier government. Sergei Shoigu, the defense minister, described them as a new form of warfare, no less dangerous for being waged with placards instead of tanks. State television carried the same message night after night: democracy promotion was a cover for encirclement, and every protest in a post-Soviet capital was a rehearsal for a protest in Moscow.

There was a self-interested logic to this view, but it was not only cynical. The men in the Kremlin had built their careers in the security services. They understood power as something taken and held, and they had seen a Soviet Union collapse from within when its leaders lost the will to use force. They believed, sincerely, that the United States was doing to Russia's neighbors what the Soviet Union had once done to Eastern Europe in reverse: pulling them, one by one, into a hostile orbit. NATO expansion in 1999 and 2004 had already brought the alliance to the Baltic coast. Now Ukraine and Georgia, the two largest non-Russian republics of the old Soviet Union, seemed to be slipping the same way.

What unsettled the Kremlin most was not the geopolitical map but the domestic one. If crowds in Kyiv could overturn a rigged election, crowds in Moscow might one day try the same. The Russian opposition was small and divided, but its activists studied the Serbian and Georgian playbooks closely, and the Kremlin knew it. From 2005 onward, foreign NGOs working inside Russia found their lives increasingly difficult. Laws on protest tightened. Funding from abroad was treated as evidence of treason in waiting.

The decade that followed would be defined by Russia's answer to a question the color revolutions had posed: what happens when a neighbor stops being obedient.

Georgia 2008, Crimea 2014

The first answer came in August 2008. The trigger was small, as such triggers often are. South Ossetia, a tiny breakaway region of Georgia, had been a frozen conflict since the early 1990s, garrisoned by Russian peacekeepers and run by a separatist administration that depended on Moscow for almost everything. Georgia's president, Mikheil Saakashvili, who had come to power on the back of the Rose Revolution, had been openly campaigning for NATO membership. At the Bucharest summit four months earlier, the alliance had declined to put Georgia on a formal path to membership but had stated, in a phrase that would be quoted for years, that Georgia and Ukraine "will become" members.

In early August, after weeks of skirmishes and shelling along the South Ossetian line, Saakashvili ordered an assault on the regional capital, Tskhinvali. Russian forces, already positioned and ready, poured through the Roki tunnel from the north. Within five days they had routed the Georgian army, occupied a substantial slice of Georgian territory, and forced Saakashvili to sign a ceasefire on Russia's terms. Moscow then recognized South Ossetia and Abkhazia, a second breakaway region, as independent states. No serious country except Russia followed suit, but the facts on the ground did not require recognition. Georgia's NATO bid was finished.

The war lasted less than a week. Its lessons travelled further than its battles. Western governments protested, suspended some forms of cooperation, and then, within months, began trying to restart relations. The Obama administration arrived in 2009 with a "reset." The European Union sent a fact-finding mission whose report, when it appeared, found that Georgia had fired first, even as it documented the disproportion of the Russian response. The political cost to Russia of using force on a neighbor turned out to be modest and short-lived.

Six years later, the cost would be tested again.

The Ukrainian crisis of 2013 and 2014 began over a trade agreement. Yanukovych, who had finally won the Ukrainian presidency in 2010, agreed to sign an association deal with the European Union and then, under heavy Russian pressure, refused at the last moment. Protesters returned to the Kyiv square, now called the Maidan, demanding he keep his word. The protests grew, met snipers' bullets in February 2014, and ended with Yanukovych fleeing across the border to Russia. Within days, unmarked soldiers in green uniforms appeared at the gates of Ukrainian military bases in Crimea, took control of the peninsula's roads and airports, and stood by while a hastily organized referendum produced a vote to join Russia. On 18 March 2014, Putin signed the treaty of annexation in the Kremlin.

Crimea was the first forcible redrawing of a European border since 1945. The Russian public, by every available measure, approved overwhelmingly. Putin's approval rating, which had been drifting downward, jumped above eighty percent and stayed there for years. The peninsula had been transferred from the Russian to the Ukrainian Soviet republic by Khrushchev in 1954, when such transfers were administrative, and most Russians considered it Russian in a way that no treaty could undo.

The annexation was followed by something more ambiguous. In the eastern Ukrainian regions of Donetsk and Luhansk, armed men seized government buildings, declared people's republics, and were quickly reinforced by fighters, weapons, and command structures that came from across the Russian border. The Ukrainian army, hollowed out by years of corruption, was slow to respond and then partially successful, until Russian regular units intervened in August 2014 to prevent the separatists' collapse. A negotiated ceasefire at Minsk produced a frozen line that froze imperfectly. Shelling continued for eight years. By the time it ended, roughly fourteen thousand people had been killed, most of them in the first eighteen months.

Western governments imposed sanctions, expelled Russia from the G8, and supplied Ukraine with non-lethal equipment and training.

Trade with Russia fell. The ruble dropped. None of it changed the situation on the ground. Crimea remained Russian. The Donbas remained contested. The frozen conflict was, for Moscow, a tool: a permanent obstacle to any Ukrainian aspiration to join NATO, since no alliance would admit a country with an active war on its territory. Putin had found, or thought he had found, the formula.

Navalny and the New Repression

Inside Russia, the years after Crimea were the years of Alexei Navalny.

He was a lawyer by training, a blogger by vocation, and a politician by sheer persistence. He had begun in the late 2000s by buying small numbers of shares in state-owned companies and using shareholder rights to demand information about how their money was spent. The information, when he got it, was damning. He published it on a blog that grew into an investigative organization, the Anti-Corruption Foundation, which over the next decade produced film after film about the palaces and yachts and bank accounts of the Russian elite.

The films were watched by tens of millions of people on YouTube. The most famous of them, released in early 2021, documented an enormous compound on the Black Sea coast that Navalny's team identified as a private residence built for Putin himself. The Kremlin denied it. The denial was not believed.

Navalny's politics were not easily classified. He had flirted with Russian nationalism in his early years, marched with the far right, and made comments about migrants from the Caucasus that his liberal allies found difficult to defend. By the 2010s he had moved toward a broader anti-corruption platform that could plausibly speak for almost everyone who was not benefiting from the system. He ran for mayor of Moscow in 2013 and, against an incumbent backed by every administrative resource the state could muster, won twenty-seven percent of the vote. He was barred from the presidential ballot in 2018 on the basis of a fraud conviction that the European Court of Human Rights had ruled politically motivated.

In August 2020, on a flight from Tomsk to Moscow, Navalny collapsed in agony. The plane made an emergency landing, and he was eventually flown to Berlin, where German doctors identified the poison as Novichok, a military-grade nerve agent produced only by Russian state laboratories. He survived. From his hospital bed, working with the investigative outlet Bellingcat, he traced the operation to specific officers of the Federal Security Service and even called one of them on the telephone, posing as an aide, and got him to describe how the poison had been applied to his underwear.

In January 2021 Navalny flew back to Moscow. He was arrested at passport control. The protests that followed were the largest Russia had seen in years, and they were crushed with a thoroughness that the protests of 2011 and 2012 had not been. Thousands were detained. Navalny himself was sent to a penal colony, then to a stricter one, then to a colony above the Arctic Circle. In February 2024 the Russian prison service announced that he had died there. He was forty-seven.

The repression that closed around him closed around everyone else too. The Anti-Corruption Foundation was declared an extremist organization, which meant that donating to it or sharing its videos could bring a prison sentence. Memorial, the human rights group that had documented Soviet-era crimes for more than thirty years, was ordered shut down by court decision at the end of 2021. Independent media outlets were branded "foreign agents," a designation that required them to attach a lengthy warning label to every publication and which most found commercially impossible to survive. By 2022 the surviving independent journalists had mostly left the country. The Russia of the 2020s was no longer the managed, semi-pluralist authoritarianism of Putin's first decade. It was something harder.

The Invasion of Ukraine

The order was given in the small hours of 24 February 2022. Russian missiles struck Ukrainian airfields, command posts, and air defense radars across the country. Armored columns crossed the border from Belarus in the north, from Russia in the east, and from occupied Crimea in the south. A helicopter assault landed at Hostomel airfield outside Kyiv, where elite Russian paratroopers expected to seize a runway and fly in reinforcements within hours. The Ukrainian capital, the planners assumed, would fall within days.

Almost nothing went according to plan. The paratroopers at Hostomel were pinned down and the airfield rendered unusable. The armored columns advancing on Kyiv stretched into the now-famous traffic jam on the road from Belarus, where Russian tanks ran out of fuel and were picked off by Ukrainian drones and ambushes. Volodymyr Zelensky, the Ukrainian president whom Russian intelligence had reportedly assessed as likely to flee, posted a video of himself in central Kyiv with the words "we are here." The capital held. By the end of March, Russian forces had withdrawn from the north entirely, leaving behind, in the suburb of Bucha and elsewhere, evidence of mass killings of civilians that would form the basis of war crimes investigations.

The war then settled into its longer shape. Russia consolidated its hold on a strip of southern and eastern Ukrainian territory connecting Crimea to the Donbas, and in September 2022 announced the annexation of four Ukrainian regions, parts of which it did not actually control. Ukrainian counteroffensives that autumn pushed the Russians out of Kharkiv region and out of the city of Kherson. After that the lines moved more slowly, and by the third year of the war they were moving in the Russian direction again, town by town, at enormous human cost.

The casualty figures defy precision but not order of magnitude. Independent estimates by Western intelligence services put Russian military deaths in the hundreds of thousands and Ukrainian deaths somewhat lower but still catastrophic for a country of forty million. Millions of Ukrainians left their homes. Whole cities, Mariupol most completely, were destroyed.

What the war revealed about Russia was as striking as what it revealed about Ukraine. The Russian army, long assumed to be the second most capable on earth, proved poorly led, poorly supplied, and dependent for its sustained operations on the mobilization of convicts, on the Wagner private military company, and eventually on a partial mobilization of ordinary Russians that triggered the largest exodus of working-age men in modern Russian history. The Wagner group's leader, Yevgeny Prigozhin, after months of public feuding with the defense ministry, launched a mutiny in June 2023, marched his troops toward Moscow, turned back at the last moment, and died two months later when his private jet fell out of the sky.

The economic war ran alongside the military one. The United States, the European Union, and their allies imposed the most extensive sanctions ever applied to a major economy. Russian central bank reserves held abroad were frozen. Major Russian banks were cut off from the international payments system. Western companies, from McDonald's to BP, withdrew. The Russian economy did not collapse, as some in the West had predicted. It reoriented toward China, India, and Turkey, sold its oil at a discount to buyers who would take it, and ran a war economy of accelerated military production and rising real wages in the defense sector. The cost was deferred rather than escaped: capital flight, brain drain, technological isolation, and a state budget increasingly devoted to the war.

Europe responded in ways that surprised even its own leaders. Germany announced a hundred-billion-euro rearmament program and began weaning itself from Russian gas. Finland and Sweden, neutral for generations, applied to join NATO and were admitted. Ukraine, which Putin had invaded in part to keep out of NATO, became more deeply tied to Western military structures than at any point in its history. The alliance Russia had wanted to push back instead grew, lengthened its border with Russia by some thirteen hundred kilometers, and recovered a sense of purpose it had not had since the end of the Cold War.

Russia and the World That Comes Next

What kind of country Russia will be when the guns stop is a question no one in Moscow can answer with confidence, and no one outside it should pretend to.

The war has remade the Russian state in ways that will outlast Putin. The security services have absorbed functions that once belonged to courts, parliaments, and the press. The defense industry has become the largest single employer in dozens of regions. A generation of young Russians has either left the country or learned to keep its opinions to itself. The educated middle class that built Moscow's restaurants and tech startups in the 2010s is scattered across Yerevan, Tbilisi, Istanbul, Belgrade, and Berlin, with no clear path home. The hardliners who pushed for the invasion have been disappointed by its conduct but vindicated in their assumption that the West would not, in the end, fight Russia directly.

The world Russia faces is also different. The unipolar moment that Putin railed against for two decades is over, but not because Russia ended it. China ended it. Russia's relationship with Beijing, declared in February 2022 to have "no limits," has become the defining external fact of Russian foreign policy: a partnership in which Russia is the junior member, supplying energy and raw materials in exchange for the manufactured goods and electronic components that sanctions deny it from the West. The pre-1991 Soviet relationship with China, in which Moscow was the senior partner and Beijing the supplicant, has been reversed within a single generation.

The smaller post-Soviet states have drawn their own conclusions. Kazakhstan, whose president sent Russian peacekeepers home within days of receiving them in 2022, has refused to recognize the annexations in Ukraine and has begun trading with greater care between its neighbors. Armenia, abandoned by Russia in its 2023 confrontation with Azerbaijan over Nagorno-Karabakh, has turned toward the European Union. The Baltic states, long warning of what Russia might do, have been vindicated in a way that gives them no pleasure. Belarus, which lent its territory to the invasion, has become more dependent on Moscow than at any time since the Soviet collapse.

Inside Russia, the older arguments continue beneath the surface. Is the country a European nation that lost its way, or a Eurasian civilization that was right to refuse Europe? Is the empire its glory or its curse? Are the Russians a people uniquely capable of suffering, as so many of their writers have claimed, or have they simply been governed badly for a very long time? These questions have been asked since the time of Peter, and they will be asked after Putin is gone.

For now, the soldiers are still in the trenches, and the drones are still flying, and the lights still burn late in the offices of the Kremlin where men plan the next move. Somewhere in a colony above the Arctic Circle there is an unmarked grave. Somewhere in Mariupol there is a building with no roof. Somewhere in a Berlin apartment a Russian journalist is writing, in Russian, for readers she will probably never meet in person. The country goes on, as it always has, larger and stranger and less finished than any single chapter of its history can contain.

The country goes on, larger and stranger and less finished than any single chapter can contain. A thousand years of it have been compressed into the pages now closing, and the compression has done what compression always does: it has left things out. Some of what was left out was unknown. Some was unknowable. Some was simply chosen against, in favor of other things. Before the book ends, the reader is owed an account of how any of this can be known at all, of which sources were trusted and which were read against the grain, and of where to go next.

Note on Sources
How We Know What We Know

The evidence for a thousand years of Russian history is uneven. For the earliest centuries it is thin and partisan, filtered through monks who wrote with one eye on the prince paying for the parchment. For the imperial period it grows dense with state paper, diplomatic dispatches, private letters, and the first serious newspapers. For the Soviet century it is at once overwhelming and treacherous: the regime documented itself obsessively, but much of what it produced was lies that the historian must learn to read against the grain. The opening of the archives after 1991 transformed the field, then partly closed again after 2000. What follows is a brief account of how this book was assembled and where its foundations are firmest.

On Methodology

The earliest narrative of Rus comes from the Primary Chronicle, compiled in Kiev in the early twelfth century from older monastic notes and oral tradition. It is the source for almost everything we think we know about Rurik, the conversion of Vladimir, and the dynastic quarrels of the first Riurikid princes. It is also a work of theology and dynastic justification, written centuries after the events it describes. Modern medievalists treat it as one source among several, cross-checked against Byzantine accounts, Arab geographers like Ibn Fadlan, Scandinavian sagas, and the archaeological record of trading sites along the Volga and Dnieper. Where these agree, we have something close to firm ground. Where they diverge, the cautious historian says so.

The Mongol period is documented mainly from outside: Persian chroniclers in the service of the Ilkhanate, papal envoys like John of Plano Carpini, and the chronicles of the surviving Russian towns. Muscovite history from the fourteenth century onward rests on a growing body of grand-princely records, monastery archives, and the diplomatic correspondence preserved by the Ambassadorial Office. By the time of Ivan IV the documentary base is rich enough to support real biography, though the tsar's own letters - including his famous exchange with the exiled Prince Kurbsky - are themselves disputed texts whose authenticity scholars have debated for decades.

The imperial archives, founded in their modern form under Peter and expanded under his successors, are the backbone of any serious history from 1700 onward. Diplomatic papers, military records, the files of the Third Section and later the Okhrana, ministerial correspondence, the census of 1897, the records of the zemstvos and the Duma - all of this survives in quantity. So do private papers: the letters of Catherine II to Voltaire and Grimm, the diaries of Nicholas II, the memoirs of ministers and generals and revolutionaries written in exile after 1917. The challenge here is not scarcity but selection.

The Soviet record is a separate problem. The Bolsheviks inherited the tsarist habit of paperwork and intensified it. Every party meeting, every denunciation, every interrogation, every quota report generated files. Much of this material was sealed for decades and became accessible only in the 1990s, when researchers like Stephen Kotkin, Anne Applebaum, and a generation of Russian historians at Memorial gained access to the central party archive, the NKVD operational files, and the records of the Gulag administration. The result was a revolution in our understanding of collectivization, the Terror, and the camps. Numbers that had been guessed at for half a century could finally be checked. Some guesses held up; others did not.

That window has narrowed. Since the early 2000s, and sharply since 2014 and again since 2022, Russian state archives have grown harder to use. Memorial, the organization that did more than any other to document Stalinist repression, was liquidated by court order in late 2021. Foreign scholars have lost visas; Russian colleagues have lost jobs or left the country. For the most recent decades the historian relies increasingly on leaked materials, investigative journalism, sanctions filings, the work of organizations like Bellingcat, and the testimony of exiles. This is not the same kind of evidence as a signed Politburo protocol, and the prudent reader should treat conclusions about Putin-era decision-making as provisional.

Russian history has always been contested terrain, fought over by nationalists, liberals, Marxists, emigres, and Western Sovietologists, each with their own canon and their own villains. This book has tried to follow the documentary evidence where it leads and to flag the places where reasonable historians still disagree. Where the sources are silent, so is the narrative.

Chronology

- **862** - According to the Primary Chronicle, the Varangian prince Rurik is invited to rule in Novgorod, traditional founding date of the Russian state.

- **988** - Prince Vladimir of Kiev converts to Eastern Christianity, binding Rus to Byzantium.

- **1237-1240** - Mongol armies under Batu Khan devastate the cities of Rus and impose two centuries of overlordship.

- **1380** - Dmitry Donskoy defeats the Mongols at Kulikovo Field, marking the rise of Moscow.

- **1547** - Ivan IV is crowned the first Tsar of all Russia.

- **1613** - Michael Romanov is elected tsar, ending the Time of Troubles and founding a dynasty that lasts until 1917.

- **1703** - Peter the Great founds St. Petersburg on the Neva delta.

- **1762** - Catherine II takes the throne in a palace coup against her husband.

- **1812** - Napoleon invades Russia; the burning of Moscow and the winter retreat destroy the Grand Army.

- **1861** - Tsar Alexander II emancipates the serfs.

- **1905** - Bloody Sunday and revolution force Nicholas II to grant a constitution and parliament.

- **1917** - The February Revolution overthrows the Romanovs; in October the Bolsheviks seize power.

- **1922** - The Union of Soviet Socialist Republics is formally established.

- **1932-1933** - Stalin's forced collectivization triggers famine across Ukraine and Kazakhstan, killing millions.

- **1937-1938** - The Great Terror peaks, with mass executions and arrests across Soviet society.

- **1941-1945** - The Great Patriotic War costs the USSR roughly 27 million lives and ends with Soviet troops in Berlin.

- **1956** - Khrushchev denounces Stalin's crimes in his Secret Speech to the 20th Party Congress.

- **1961** - Yuri Gagarin becomes the first human in space.

- **1979** - Soviet forces invade Afghanistan, beginning a decade-long war.

- **1986** - The Chernobyl nuclear reactor explodes, exposing the failings of the Soviet system.

- **1991** - After a failed August coup, the Soviet Union is dissolved on December 25.

- **1999-2000** - Vladimir Putin becomes prime minister, then acting president, then elected president.

- **2014** - Russia annexes Crimea and foments war in eastern Ukraine.

- **2022** - Russia launches a full-scale invasion of Ukraine, triggering the largest war in Europe since 1945.

Further Reading

The literature on Russia in English is enormous and growing. The titles below are the ones a curious reader could pick up next and trust. They include surveys, focused monographs, biography, and reporting; together they cover the ground this book has crossed at speed.

- **Geoffrey Hosking, Russia and the Russians: A History (2001).** The best single-volume survey of Russian history from the medieval period to the post-Soviet era.

- **Janet Martin, Medieval Russia, 980-1584 (2007).** The standard scholarly survey of the period from Kievan Rus through Ivan the Terrible.

- **Simon Sebag Montefiore, The Romanovs: 1613-1918 (2016).** A vivid dynastic history that brings three centuries of tsars to life.

- **Dominic Lieven, Russia Against Napoleon (2009).** A revisionist account of 1812 that restores Russia to the center of the story.

- **Orlando Figes, Natasha's Dance: A Cultural History of Russia (2002).** A lyrical exploration of Russian identity through art, literature, and everyday life.

- **Orlando Figes, A People's Tragedy: The Russian Revolution 1891-1924 (1996).** A definitive narrative of the revolutionary era from below as well as above.

- **Robert Service, A History of Modern Russia: From Tsarism to the Twenty-First Century (2009).** Authoritative coverage of the past century by a leading biographer of Lenin, Stalin, and Trotsky.

- **Stephen Kotkin, Stalin: Paradoxes of Power, 1878-1928 (2014).** The first volume of a monumental biography that reframes Stalin and the Soviet project.

- **Anne Applebaum, Gulag: A History (2003).** A Pulitzer-winning history of the Soviet camp system based on newly opened archives.

- **Anne Applebaum, Red Famine: Stalin's War on Ukraine (2017).** Essential reading on the Holodomor and the long roots of Russia's confrontation with Ukraine.

- **Antony Beevor, Stalingrad (1998).** A gripping account of the battle that turned the Second World War.

- **Svetlana Alexievich, Secondhand Time: The Last of the Soviets (2013).** An oral history of the collapse of the USSR told in the voices of those who lived it.

- **Serhii Plokhy, The Last Empire: The Final Days of the Soviet Union (2014).** A close-up history of the months leading to the dissolution of the USSR.

- **Masha Gessen, The Future Is History: How Totalitarianism Reclaimed Russia (2017).** A National Book Award-winning portrait of post-Soviet Russia through seven lives.

- **Catherine Belton, Putin's People: How the KGB Took Back Russia and Then Took On the West (2020).** An investigative account of the security-state networks behind the Putin regime.

Beyond the books, the serious reader will want to know the primary voices: the chronicles in Samuel Cross's translation, the letters of Ivan IV and Kurbsky, the memoirs of Catherine the Great, Herzen's *My Past and Thoughts*, the diaries of Nicholas II, the speeches and writings of Lenin and Trotsky, Solzhenitsyn's *The Gulag Archipelago*, Nadezhda Mandelstam's *Hope Against Hope*, Anna Politkovskaya's reporting from Chechnya. Russian history is, among other things, a literature. Read it in the original voices wherever possible, and read more than one of them on any question that matters.

www.ingramcontent.com/pod-product-compliance
Lightning Source LLC
Chambersburg PA
CBHW071501140726
47997CB00005B/1816